Reaching Women:
The way to go in marketing
healthcare services

Barbara Alpern Lehman

Authors Choice Press

San Jose New York Lincoln Shanghai

Reaching Women
The way to go in marketing healthcare services

Authors Choice Press
an imprint of iUniverse.com, Inc.

For information address:
iUniverse.com, Inc.
5220 S 16th, Ste. 200
Lincoln, NE 68512
www.iuniverse.com

Originally published by Pluribus Press

ISBN: 0-595-18724-2

Printed in the United States of America

To all the clients, colleagues, and friends from whom I have been so privileged to learn so much.

Contents

ILLUSTRATIONS

All ads are reprinted with permission. The authors wish to thank the following healthcare organizations and advertising agencies for their participation:

PREFACE

Compared to the other categories of general consumer advertising, the advertising and promotion of healthcare services is in its early childhood. Scarcely six years old, this new consumer advertising thrust has had to learn a great deal in a very short time. But the child is learning fast, acquiring the skills necessary to succeed in a fiercely competitive marketplace.

Although it has borrowed liberally from knowledge gained from older, more experienced product advertising such as cosmetics and detergents, the marketing and sales promotion of healthcare has its own legal, financial and ethical constraints. These restrictions have shaped the approaches and tone of this category of advertising and have defined current healthcare advertising.

In the short, intense history of healthcare advertising, marketers have quickly learned standard advertising methodology: the necessity of market research, targeting and segmenting audiences, interpreting data, positioning techniques, communication strategy, media planning and scheduling, tracking and measuring results and, above all, the undeniable appeal of an effective creative concept. Although progress in each of these areas is uneven, varying according to geographical areas (and market demands in each region), the level of expertise of practitioners and the quality of advertising services provided have grown up and acquired new sophistication as a product category.

Healthcare marketers now are turning their attention to fine-tuning their skills. With the era of the mass market over, with so many media outlets available and with the diversity of the healthcare audience itself, marketers are faced with the task of selecting key targets for their messages. *For healthcare, that key audience is women.* Because so much is riding on it, it is absolutely essential to define women as an audience segment and address their needs.

As general consumer product advertisers know, women in the 1980s are a difficult market to pin down. "Moving targets," women are still in transition, a process that began in the 1960s. Traditional methods of identifying and interpreting demographic information are no longer applicable to this market. Much of the data is only a hint, a shadow of the full truth. It is important to be sincere and accurate in advertising to the female market. While there are a lot of women who are easily exploited, there are a growing number of women who are becoming aware and informed consumers. To deny or ignore this powerful segment is to create a potential backlash of attitudes from which a hospital service or product may never recover.

This book provides insights—beyond the statistics—into the fascinating and lucrative women's market. By understanding this potential, healthcare marketers should be able to reach and retain the female customer. By so doing, those who market healthcare to the women's audience will benefit not only their own organizations but also provide an equal, if not greater, service to the female consumer in her role as gatekeeper and guardian of health for herself and her family.

ACKNOWLEDGMENTS

Writing a book is instructive. You start out thinking it's a solitary task but learn quickly just how collaborative it is. I learned early whom I could rely upon to share this awesome responsibility.

Co-contributors Marjorie and Morton Shaevitz and Kristine Peterson were gracious enough to share this experience with me. In record time they rallied their respective areas of expertise into chapters that contributed greatly to the depth and scope of this book. I'm grateful to Marjorie and Morton Shaevitz for providing the psychological perspective of what motivates women and why, and to Kristine Peterson for her succinct analysis of how the marketing function impacts the consumer on a face-to-face basis. Each is an expert in her field, and I am most pleased they agreed to participate in this project.

My special thanks and appreciation go to Betsy Myers, my right-hand woman, whose intelligence, illumination, encouragement and cunning research capabilities assisted me throughout the development of this book. From the big picture to the last detail, her diligence has kept this project on target and on time.

Of particular importance was the patience and support I received from my partner and friend Karen York, who was always a valuable sounding board for ideas.

And I want to applaud the creative and marketing specialists who developed the various advertisements showcased in this book as well as the advertisers who stimulated their creative people to do the caliber of work this represents.

These are challenging times for women, and exciting ones as well. If this book provides an insight into the motivation of the female consumer, then I hope this book will have been of marketing as well as sociological value.

INTRODUCTION

A generation ago, there were approximately an equal number of men and women in the United States, but there are now 6.4 million more women than men, and this numerical advantage is expected to continue well into the next century. For the foreseeable future, a clear majority of the adult population as well as the majority of patients in virtually every hospital will be women.

—Peter K. Francese
American Demographics, Inc.

Women hold the majority of wealth in America and buy the majority of food, clothing and toiletries. Women represent the fastest growing population in the work force and have the most frequent encounters with healthcare all through their lives.

The growing strength and influence of women in the marketplace force us to reevaluate our marketing approach to this important segment of the population.

Along with financial services, travel companies and automobile manufacturers, healthcare marketers are "discovering" the women's role in purchase decisions. This late-blooming realization is a function of shifting demographics, the feminist movement, the age of consumerism, the single career woman, the two-paycheck family and a longer, more active life expectancy. Women's roles have changed dramatically over the last 25 years! And as the baby boomers hit 40 and come fully into their own, these changes are accelerating. Marketers in health, finance, travel, real estate and automotive have been slow to identify trends that advertisers of cosmetics, household items, groceries and fashion have recognized all along. But change is in the air, and American Express is one of the best examples of it (see exhibit I-1).

Consumer products and package goods advertisers spend millions to research their customers' needs, package their products, develop their advertising campaigns and target their media. Mass market products/services require mass market promotional efforts, and the cost is enormous.

Healthcare advertisers, with some notable exceptions in the areas of substance abuse, health plans and over-the-counter pharmaceuticals, generally are not mass-marketing oriented and have neither the budgets nor the desire to be so. But the marketing lessons learned in other industries can be adapted by them. Where this is happening, a distinctive way to market healthcare to women is emerging. Healthcare advertisers realize that the challenge is to *out-think* the competition, not just outspend it.

There is a problem, however. As we approach the 1990s, the women's market is still undergoing significant changes in numbers and, more importantly, in attitudes and values. Women's growing independence and confidence, based on the necessity or desire to earn their own dollars, is still changing the rules of the game for advertisers. Mothers are encouraging their daughters to study more math in school, to attend business classes, manage their own finances and pursue whatever professional goals they choose, regardless of gender stereotypes. There is a new generation of independent women of all ages emerging, and the only

Exhibit I-1

constant in the women's market is change.

WOMEN AND HEALTHCARE

The Florida Hospital ad recognizes how far women have come in not settling for traditional careers (see exhibit I-2).

Against the background of strength women exert in the general consumer marketplace, women play an even stronger role in healthcare purchases. A recent study shows that at least 65 percent of all healthcare purchases are made or influenced by women!

While they may not yet make the primary decision about which wrench to buy or what oil filter to use, women do select the family physician, their own OB/GYN, their children's pediatrician, their parent's nursing home and their spouse's physician. They buy and dispense the medicines, decide when it's time to seek a second medical opinion, look for outside help with family or marital problems and enroll themselves or family members in behavioral programs. And, since so many are now in the work force, women also decide which health plan to use.

Even in the most male-dominated families, it is often the woman who gathers the necessary information, appears in the health facility waiting rooms and presents the health-related issues or problems, as she sees them.

Women are accustomed to dealing with sickness, infirmity, pain, old age and death. From the onset of menstruation through childbirth, yearly pap smears, coping with children's illnesses and accommodating aging parents, women earn their quasi-medical stripes. These life experiences raise their familiarity with healthcare problems—much more than for men.

As gatekeepers to an entire range of healthcare services, it's a mistake to assume women are only fair targets for obstetrics, gynecology and pediatrics. Women choose emergency departments, walk-in clinics, hospitals, alcohol treatment programs and retirement or long-term care accommodations.

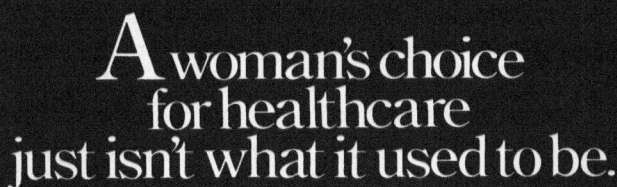

Exhibit I-2

Combine this with women's growing knowledge about health issues, popularized by the mass media, higher educational level and experience in the workaday world and it's clear why women are indeed powerful gatekeepers. Even for impotency clinics and cardiac rehabilitation programs, traditionally male dominated, women constitute a significant and influential audience and must be included in the marketing message.

HEALTHCARE AS A BUSINESS

The healthcare field is referred to more and more as an "industry" or "business," a nomenclature which has met with considerable resistance by health professionals and public alike. Health, like religion, is supposed to be beyond the exigencies of operating budgets, cost containment and market share, according to traditional thought. But slowly, painfully, healthcare is having to accept the fact that it is a business after all. As such, in order to thrive and not merely survive, healthcare must look to the marketplace, assess the needs and requirements of the many audiences it hopes to serve, and redefine, restructure or repackage its services in order to meet those marketplace demands. Competition, deregulation and legislation have made it so.

Let's deal with the implications first. Healthcare marketers must:

■ Respond to change pro-actively.

Change is always discomforting, but when the stakes are as high as they are in healthcare, marketers must learn to accept, cope and move to take advantage of this knowledge. Nowhere is this more applicable than in the ever-changing women's market.

■ Be more sensitive to the three levels of issues that are meaningful to women: those from society at large, those in their communities and those in their own lives. Not all women are at the same psychological place at the same time. Women in a small town may be where women in a large cosmopolitan city were 10 years ago vis-a-vis their view of themselves and their place in the world. Similarly, there are generational differences. Women in their 20s take feminism for granted; women in their 40s are still challenging the turf. Women in their 50s face different kinds of challenges and choices than women in their 60s did a decade ago.

- Be keenly aware of the incredible complexity of the women's market.

It is not enough to target "women" as an audience. As examined throughout this book, "women" cannot be lumped into any one category. All 35-year-old married women are not the same. Some may have children or a career or both. Some women have advanced degrees and do not work, while others have only a high school education and are employed. The very fact that so many segments exist within this audience means that marketers may need to do "niche" marketing, carefully aiming their message at specific women with psychological or lifestyle similarities. It may be that a particular healthcare service is not appropriate for some audiences, that another may prove more profitable to pursue.

- Be aware of certain common denominators that link all women—regardless of their time, place or situation.

These unifying themes appeal to every woman. Discussed in greater depth further on, these common denominators provide some essential starting points for creating successful marketing and advertising plans.

To take advantage of this competitive environment, healthcare marketers must:

- Assume greater risks in advertising. Women are subjected to several thousand advertising messages daily. Not only must an organization's healthcare advertising compete for attention among the dozens of other healthcare messages but it also must fight against the general consumer "noise level" of other product and service advertising. Therefore, the program concept, marketing strategy and advertising must be distinctive. New approaches, new channels and new creative ad concepts mean navigating uncharted waters that, within the bounds of good taste and ethics, are going to make that organization's advertising stand out from the crowd and be memorable.

- Budget enough money for promotion and research to achieve a professional level of quality and then hire internal and external support who are experienced and competent. Developing a comprehensive advertising plan, based on sound market research, determining a well-defined corporate mission and establishing an underlying theme are not piecemeal processes thrown together by an organization. (Or ripped apart by competing factions within it!) "Survival marketing" involves firm top executive authority that can mobilize all departments to speak with *one voice.* And it involves commitment of key executives to allocate a budget sufficient to meet the challenge.

- Realize that marketing and advertising are ongoing costs of doing business, not short-term reactions to impulse. Sporadic, short-term advertising is neither efficient nor effective. Enough resources, time and talent must be expended to meet goals, assess the results and make adjustments as needed. Marketing to women is a process of building awareness, name recognition, image and trust. Attaining that goal takes time and continuous, consistent effort. Often years of both.

If an organization is committed to capturing and retaining the loyalty of the women's market, then it has to commit the funds necessary over time to build those loyalties.

- Build a consensus to be able to move quickly and decisively. Too often, the most acutely delineated marketing plans, the most painstaking marketing research and the most compelling advertisements are developed, only to become bogged down in the politics of the organization or the sudden discovery that too little money is allocated to accomplish the goals. What lies at the heart of this glitch is fear—fear of losing one's job, fear of not being promoted, fear of failure, fear of the vulnerability that increased visibility will bring. For all these reasons and more, top management should be involved in the project from the onset—and all the way through. A consensus must be built and sustained throughout the marketing process. And the responsibility, for better or for worse, lies with the marketing director. He or she must have the authority and willingness to assume the responsibility for an actionable plan—or the objective is lost before it gets started. (See "An Action Plan" at the end of this chapter.)

THE BOTTOM LINE

Effectively advertising to women requires imaginative marketing skills. Those who take the time to find out what women need, how they want to learn about healthcare and what will satisfy their needs (once they are sufficiently interested) will be rewarded. A vast marketplace, a wealth of opportunities within it and the potential for return on investment, make marketing to women, as challenging and demanding as it is, well worth the effort. American Express thinks so too.

An Action Plan

The following chart and timetable demonstrates how to create and implement a typical marketing plan. This chart also assumes:

1. The marketing specialist has the authority as well as responsibility from top executive management.

2. There is a known and endorsed mission statement.

3. The budget is realistic and flexible enough to respond to market fluctuations and challenges.

4. Knowledgeable and experienced advertising consultants have been selected and engaged to assist and advise the client through the process.

5. A financial and psychological commitment of six months to a year has been made to allow sufficient time to assess the results of the program and measure its cost-effectiveness.

Write Marketing Plan—Two–three months

The marketing plan should assess the competitive factors, include all relevant research about the target market(s), outline the program elements, create a projected budget based on revenues expected and costs anticipated, specify and assign program responsibilities, define the market position and current market share of the organization's proposed service, and finally, set one major objective and several quantifiable goals.

Conduct Market Research—Two–three months

Market research and the need for it is discussed in a later chapter. The results and interpretation of this research should be written in a report and copies distributed to key personnel. At this point, a thorough evaluation of the findings should be made and the value of the project squared with the organization's objectives. It may be, for example, that the research indicates that too few women would be either available or interested in the projected service, that its potential revenue is insufficient for the time and expense necessary to promote it. Or it may be revealed that the service is inappropriate to the organization, or that the initial marketing plan contradicts the referral or healthcare usage patterns in the community. Market research may also indicate unforeseen opportunities in other areas of service or that a different type of campaign or organizational restructuring is needed.

Prepare Advertising Plan—One month

By now, considerable information has been assembled. It should be fully shared with the advertising agency, good news and bad. Your agency will prepare a comprehensive advertising and promotional plan, media schedule and proposed budget for review and approval. The moment of truth! Evaluate the plan in light of your objectives, assuming that the plan is budgeted appropriately for the task.

If the budget is higher than you can justify, yet the plan is sound, list the elements by priority and determine which ones can be phased in over time.

Seek agreement of the modified plan.

Creation and Approval of Materials— Two–six months, depending

While the agency is preparing its materials, advertisers sometimes experience "buyer's remorse" and become apprehensive. The lull in the active role marketers have played up to this point creates a certain level of discomfort. If your agency is tuned in to your need for action, your anxiety will pass as each piece of the puzzle falls into place.

And, for your part, be accessible to agency personnel, to speed the process when decisions must be made.

Tracking/Measurement—Ongoing

Let's assume the ads for your campaign have appeared, the brochures printed and distributed, and the program is underway. Don't sit by the phone or the cash register. Remember, healthcare is not an impulse purchase. You seek long-term relationships, not one-night stands. The program staff should keep records to track the source of responses. These may be in the form of telephone inquiries, mail-in coupons, number of appointments made and kept, and revenue produced. The records will be compiled into daily, weekly and monthly reports for review for the duration of the advertising campaign.

Post-Market Research—Three–six months into the campaign

A formal study should be made of the use and acceptance of the program by its key audience, measured against its goals. For instance, an image campaign survey will measure awareness and perception, while a traffic-building campaign will measure service satisfaction and preference.

Evaluation—Ongoing

Quarterly evaluations should be made by the senior staff to assess the research results and evaluate the campaign: did it achieve the goals for which it was designed?

Modification—After post-market research has been evaluated

Based on what has been learned from the experiences and results of the promotional effort, the program may be discontinued, extended or certain elements changed or added. A new advertising plan or continuation of the existing one may be indicated, and the process begins again.

WHY WOMEN CONSUMERS ARE THE WAY THEY ARE

Marjorie Hansen Shaevitz, M.A.,
with *Morton H. Shaevitz, Ph.D.*

Some years ago I was in a large mid-Western city appearing on a morning television show as part of a book promotion media tour. The producers of the show had brought in a 35-year-old local woman to join me in talking about the subject of a book that I had just written, *The Superwoman Syndrome.*

Before the program began, the other guest and I were asked to wait in the television "green room" area. As soon as we sat down, the woman (we'll call her Jan) began talking. She said rather pointedly,

"Marjorie, I just want to let you know that I'm *not* a superwoman."

I wasn't surprised by her remark. I had found that many women felt that it was demeaning to be labeled a "superwoman." So I congratulated Jan and told her that I was delighted to hear that she hadn't fallen victim to the super-woman "do it all" mythology.

"Right," she said, "I'm not a superwoman, but I will have to admit that I have been exhausted for the past four years!"

I smiled to myself as she continued.

"To begin with, I am the mother of four children—all under the age of six! I work part-time for an airline, but I work on-call. My husband is a hard-working executive with one of the city's big business firms, and he rarely gets home before 9:00 p.m. By that time, of course, the children are usually asleep. Oh, and my father is in a local hospital dying of cancer. As a matter of fact, for the past three nights I've been sleeping on the floor of his hospital room because he 'could go' at any time."

I nodded in sympathy as this perfectly coiffed, "dressed for success" woman talked on.

"Of course, I am tired most of the time. I have been to see all kinds of doctors over the past few years to help me with this exhaustion problem. In fact, just last week I had a full medical workup, tests and all. To tell you the truth, I was really hoping that they would find something wrong with me . . . you know, a minor thyroid problem or some kind of vitamin deficiency. I was really *disappointed* when the doctor told me everything was 'just fine.' In fact, he said I had a 'clean bill of health.'"

By this time Jan had tears in her eyes. I could see the frustration on her face.

"I really hate going to doctors! When they don't find anything wrong, they treat me like I'm crazy. I know there is something wrong! Why else would I feel the way I do? You know, I was hoping so much that this last doctor would find something wrong with me because then maybe he could give me some medicine to feel better, or maybe he would tell me to stop working so hard."

What's going on here? What does Jan tell us about women today? How does her story reflect what is going on in healthcare? How did Jan's physician react to her apparent lack of enthusiasm about having a "clean bill of health"? What does this woman need from the healthcare system that she didn't get? What did she get instead?

Let's look at Jan, the typical woman of today, and see how she exemplifies what we should know about women healthcare consumers.

Like many women, Jan is a mix of the past and present. Just as her mother took major responsibility for the care of her family (including her Dad), so does Jan. But she is also dealing with the new stresses of being a working woman. Moreover, she is "in transition," working part-time until (she told me) "the youngest child is in school."

Jan is completely overwhelmed with her responsibilities and has defined her problem as a physical one—exhaustion—and has been seeking medical help. Having been told over and over that "everything is just fine," Jan feels confused, disappointed and frustrated. Needless to say, her problem hasn't been solved—her symptoms persist, and her needs have not been addressed. As we shall see, this is quite consistent with how scores of other women face this dilemma.

WHAT THIS CHAPTER IS ALL ABOUT

In this chapter I will examine what I see as the major contemporary issues facing women in the 80s. First, we'll take a look at some recent demographic information. Then, I'll identify the issues that you as health professionals should be aware of in providing direct services to women. Next, I'll describe some of the concerns and needs of today's women that you might want to address programmatically, that is, by offering educational programs and seminars, putting together resource materials, or developing information centers.

To explain how today's women have evolved, I'll describe

contemporary and historical forces that have been pressing on them, specifically, socialization factors and cultural changes. Finally, I'll make some recommendations on how you might improve the process of addressing women's consumer needs.

WOMEN TODAY

Here are some surprising statistics collected from the Bureau of the Census, commissions on the status of women, and other current sources. Both the recent statistics as well as some of the historical data that accompanies them will provide a realistic perspective of contemporary American women.

1. *Jan is one of a large number of women who is joining the national labor force and who will probably remain there for most of her lifetime.* As of 1983, the total population of the U.S. was 234 million.[1] Women made up 53 percent of that total population and 45 percent of the American labor force.[2] In 1950, women made up only 29 percent of the work force.[3] As of 1984, 63 percent of all American women were in the labor force.[4] Eighty percent of these women were employed full-time.[5] An article in the *Los Angeles Herald Examiner* recently predicted that only one out of ten women now living will never work outside the home.[6]

2. *Like Jan, the vast majority of employed women work in non-professional, high stress, low satisfaction occupations.* Of all employed women in 1985, 77 percent were in non-professional occupations: clerical, sales, service, factory or plant jobs.[7] Women account for 99 percent of secretaries, 97 percent of typists, and 96 percent of all registered nurses.[8]

Only 11 percent of women workers are in non-traditional occupations (those in which 75 percent or more of the workers are men).

Twenty-three percent of the female work force are in managerial and professional occupations, but the majority of

women professional workers (59 percent) are in two traditionally female jobs—teaching and nursing.[9]

3. *Most women work out of economic necessity and earn low
salaries.* Seventy percent of today's working women are single, widowed, divorced, or married to men who earn less than
$15,000 a year or unemployed.[10] Fifty-one percent of female
workers earn less than $15,000 a year (compared to 28 per-
cent of men);[11] 25 percent of female workers earn less than
$10,000 a year.[12] *The average income for single, working
mothers is $9,000 a year.*[13]

Among some physicians, the perception has been that
women entered the work force for personal growth or self-
fulfillment reasons. However, as the statistics show, most
women have gone to work because they or their families
needed the money. The combined forces of inflation and reces-
sion have put incredible pressures on American families,
particularly those headed by women.

Needless to say, these women—who may need health
services the most—often feel that they have neither the
time nor the resources to afford them. They are unlikely can-
didates for optional, nonreimbursable services and programs such as preventive health, screening mammograms,
or annual physicals.

4. *Very few women are part of the elite, executive group that is
so often described in popular magazines and newspapers.* Ten
percent of employed women earn more than $20,000 a year,[14]
and 6 percent earn over $30,000 a year (compared to 25 per-
cent of men).[15] Only 60,000 women—one-tenth of one
percent—who work outside the home earn over $75,000 a
year.[16] Women earn, on the average, 64¢ for every $1.00
earned by men.[17]

Women who have financial resources are highly selective
consumers and will choose delivery systems that recognize and
cater to their specialized needs. Among other things, they

want convenience; high quality; professional, respectful treatment; the most advanced procedures and technology; lots of information; attractive surroundings; and a sense that their time is as valuable as the health care providers'. Jan is still looking for such a system.

5. *As they age, the ratio of women to men increases dramatically.* According to the U.S. Bureau of Census, in the under-20 age group the 1980 census found 35.5 million women versus 37 million men. The 20-24 year age group was evenly balanced at about 10.7 million each. But for the 65 years of age and older group, there were 15.2 million women and 10.2 million men, and the disparity is even more marked in the upper age ranges.

Because women tend to marry younger and outlive men, most elderly women and widows live alone and most elderly men live with their wives. Women 65 years and older constitute the fastest growing segment of the population.[18]

By offering services and programs that meet both the *physical* needs (i.e., prevention of osteoporosis, early signs of stroke, nutritional requirements of older adults) and *psychological* needs (i.e., widow-to-widow programs, exercise programs for health and well-being, housing and old age care alternatives, budgeting for health), a health organization increases the likelihood that this older population will choose all of their healthcare from the same facility.

6. *Even though it has become an option, most women today will still have at least one child.* By age 40, 90 percent of all American women will have had a child,[19] although this seems to be changing some now for women in their 20s and 30s. Of all women with children under the age of 18, 62.3 percent are employed (as compared to 8.5 percent in 1940, 21.6 percent in 1950, 42.9 percent in 1970, and 50 percent in 1977).[20] Fifty percent of mothers of preschool children work outside the home, while 48 percent of mothers with children under the age

of one year are employed.[21] One out of five children born in 1986 was born to an unmarried mother.[22]

With a decrease in time and an increase in responsibilities, some women will look for healthcare settings that can respond to children's healthcare needs in the least complicated ways for the mother.

7. *Half of all married women will go through a divorce, and almost all children of divorce remain with the mother.* While in 1940 there was one divorce for every six marriages, in 1980 there was one divorce for every two marriages.[23] *The Wall Street Journal* acknowledges that this trend is continuing into the mid-eighties.[24] Sixty percent of divorced women are single parents, and the prospects for their remarrying are bleak. Only 18 percent of divorced women eventually remarry.[25] Fifty percent of the children born in the 1980s will go through a divorce, and 90 percent of those who get divorced will end up living with their mother.[26]

For single mothers, good child care is an almost impossible dream, though the need is an everyday, painful reality. Unless she has exceptional skill at choosing a child care resource, or is unusually lucky, the chances of a mother finding quality long-term child care are slim. In many cases, child care is simply not available. Many single mothers take whatever or whoever is around. There are 23 million children in our country who need child care because their mothers work, but there are only 1.2 million licensed day care slots available.[27] Little or no information is available on the "quality" of these facilities.

As a result, each single mother must act alone in determining her children's needs, setting her standards, choosing a site or person, training or evaluating that choice, and monitoring her children and the situation on a daily basis. On the private market, where and when it is available, costs range from $80 to $200 per child per week[28]—an impossible figure for women making, on the average, $9,000 a year.

Who or what provides child care is a critical decision

because of the length of time children spend with them and the impact they have.

Healthcare providers wishing to address this question for single mothers (thereby developing a consumer awareness of their organizations) can provide low cost or no cost programs which educate mothers about how to choose and evaluate child care centers for children at various ages. Another way of developing consumer awareness is for the organization to sponsor single parenting classes.

Some forward-looking healthcare groups are providing after-hour and weekend appointments and services for this segment of the population and a few are even developing day care for sick children. "Sniffles Rooms" for contagious and non-contagious illnesses are mushrooming all over the country to aid desperate mothers in one of their times of greatest need.

8. *Women are working as many, if not longer, hours per week than at any other time.* According to economist Sylvia Ann Hewlett, the typical American woman's work week is 21 hours longer than that of their male counterpart.[29] She further asserts that American men do less than a quarter of all household tasks—despite the massive shift of their wives or partners into paid employment! Men's average time devoted to family work has increased by only 6 percent in the past 20 years.[30] Another economist, Heidi Hartmann, claims that men actually demand eight hours *more* service per week than they contribute.[31]

The implication of this is that many American women are exhausted! Like Jan, many women have accepted as normal an overwhelming, non-stop lifestyle. And they often go to physicians for help. At this point, few physicians know how to provide it—or even know of a referral source that will.

Aside from treating specific health conditions and diseases usually associated with women (maternity and gynecological issues, diseases of the breast, plastic surgery, and genito-urinary conditions), what other contemporary problems should your health organization be aware of?

WOMEN'S ISSUES THAT HAVE IMPLICATIONS FOR DIRECT SERVICES

1. *Whether she is single or married, has children or not, works outside the home or is a volunteer, a great many American women describe their lives as out-of-control and overwhelming.* Finding time to do what they think they must is a major pressure. Unlike men, who continue to see their major role as that of family breadwinner, women feel pulled in multiple directions. They feel responsible to husbands (or "significant others"), children, parents and in-laws, friends, other family members, employers or employees, colleagues, even casual acquaintances. And their behavior demonstrates this in their fragmented, unending involvement with those people. Therefore, healthcare organizations that ignore women's hectic lifestyles—those which offer limited hours, inconvenient locations, unsupportive staff, uninformed physicians, long waiting periods—only add to their stress and pressure.

2. *Because of their particular socialization patterns, women rarely address their own needs for care, rest, or relaxation except when they're ill.* In most women's minds, being sick is the "only excuse" for not doing . . . well, almost anything. What we find commonplace now are women pushing themselves to the state of exhaustion and illness. Fatigue as a physical symptom is a legitimate way for women to express the stress they are feeling.

Like Jan, in the beginning anecdote, many women are experiencing stress-related disorders (that is, specific physical and/or emotional symptoms, sometimes diagnosed as somatoform disorders, as a result of living demanding, pressure-filled lives). Stress, furthermore, often produces maladaptive behaviors such as obesity, eating disorders, smoking and substance abuse. Often, as was true in Jan's case, her physician found no systemic disease and she was declared "well," although she still experienced adverse symptoms. Such a situation obviously leads to further stress on the part of the patient and her ultimate distrust of the healthcare system.

Therefore, healthcare organizations which understand women's underlying need to be cared for, and which treat stress-related disorders with as much respect as organically-based afflictions, will go a long way toward treating women appropriately and meeting both their physical and emotional needs.

What Jan might have been told by her physician was this: "Now that we can rule out any major medical illness, let's see if we can find out why you feel so bad and what we can do about it."

3. *Most women are seriously concerned about money.* With more and more women working outside the home, one often gets the impression that women are experiencing fewer and fewer financial problems. Nothing could be further from the truth. The income levels of American women today are shockingly low, particularly among single mother and older woman populations. Money (or the lack of it) is the number one stress issue for the '80s woman. Therefore, women are acutely sensitive to the costs of today's healthcare.

In addition, most women consumers have had little experience with third party payees such as Blue Cross/Blue Shield and Health Maintenance Organizations. When a claim for reimbursement is refused, or only partially accepted, many women will accept the decision and then either reduce their utilization of the health system's services or switch their affiliation to another provider. Rather than being just the collector of payments, healthcare business offices need to become proactive, to help women patients with their financial problems. Indeed, the business office can become the patient's advocate in dealing with third party payees.

4. *Most women feel responsible for maintaining the health of family members, including husbands, children, parents, and in-laws.* Women choose pediatricians for their children, doctors and hospitals for their ill parents, executive health programs for their spouses. Therefore, the healthcare organizations that meet women's needs and earn their loyalty and respect can almost be assured of treating their families.

5. *As women's roles have changed so have the pressures to be attractive, fit and healthy.* Today women are concerned about exercise, weight control, plastic surgery, nutrition and disease prevention, not only for themselves but for their families too. Therefore, healthcare organization services must meet those needs to attract women as consumers.

WOMEN'S ISSUES THAT HAVE IMPLICATIONS FOR HOSPITAL PROGRAM OFFERINGS

Along with the more traditional health concerns, today's woman is also concerned about a variety of relatively new issues. Paramount among them is the necessity of *balancing a complicated lifestyle.* There are pressures, past and present, which overwhelm women in their everyday lives.

There are also unique pressures in *finding and keeping a relationship with a member of the opposite sex.* Look at the titles of books that have hit the recent bestseller lists: *Sexual Static: How Men Are Confusing the Women They Love, Women Who Love Too Much, Men Who Hate Women and the Women Who Love Them* and *Smart Women, Foolish Choices.* All address the fact that it has never been more difficult to sustain an intimate relationship. At best, most relationships between men and women are precarious and tenuous. The divorce statistics cited earlier surely substantiate this. There is also a growing anxiety about how to have "safe sex" with the advent of AIDS and the prevalence of other venereal diseases.

Because divorce is increasingly commonplace, most

women have to reckon with employment outside the home and all its attendant concerns. Except for the birth of a child (or the loss of a spouse), nothing affects a woman's life more than entering the work force. Even if she is not career oriented, the pressures on a woman to be employed are strong. For younger women, working is not enough; they feel that they must also excel in their job and achieve a high level of success. The number of "Type A" women (hard-driven, ambitious, overworked) has increased dramatically.

Women now need to find work, deal with policies and procedures developed 20, 30, or 50 years ago, develop career paths, find mentors and join network groups, and deal with job success—while also taking care of a household and a family.

In order to compete for good men and good jobs, *women must appear fit, look attractive, feel young, be active, live healthily and help those around them to do the same.*

Therefore, the healthcare organizations which provide information and programs that genuinely help women deal with these issues (at convenient times and places, and at affordable prices) will be rewarded with their patronage.

TRADITIONAL SOCIALIZATION FORCES

Whether socialization or genetic predisposition influences who we are is controversial. And, as yet, this moot point has not been resolved. However, we can say that what we inherit from our parents plays an important part in determining who we are, especially when it comes to such areas as verbal and spatial skills (girls are better at the former; boys, the latter), activity, aggressiveness and mood.

Before the early '70s, parents raised girls and boys in a straightforward manner. Few persons, if any, questioned the traditional model of raising girls to be wives, mothers and homemakers and boys to be successful breadwinners. Most parents employed both conscious and unconscious techniques for making their girls feminine and their boys masculine.

Parental socialization was then reinforced at school and in movies, magazines, newspapers, books, press—by the total culture.

In the '80s almost everyone recognizes that by treating girls one way and boys another, parents influence adult behavior and thought; but it has only been in the last few years that social scientists have delineated the different socializations experienced by boys and girls. When boys and girls are reared differently, they react, think, behave, talk, argue, and confront situations disparately as adults.

By examining some of the ways in which we raise girls, we can better understand today's women.

How Their Socialization Affects Women

The goal of traditional socialization, to reiterate, was for a girl to become a wife, mother and homemaker. The behaviors we encouraged in girls were supposed to ready them for their future home and family roles. (Conversely, the objective of traditional socialization for a boy was to become a successful worker, and the behaviors we encouraged in them were supposed to ready them for the male work world.)

How were girls encouraged to be good wives, mothers and homemakers? *Above all, they were reared to be relationship and people-oriented. Unlike boys, they were supposed to be "other" rather than self-oriented.* More than anything else, this socialized "other" orientation explains much of contemporary female behavior. Girls essentially were told to "take care" of everybody but themselves; therefore, as adults, women are predisposed to act in ways detrimental to their own health and well-being.

1. *Women generally fail to take proper physical and emotional care of themselves.* According to traditional socialization, one of the most fundamental functions of women is to nurture others. Because they have been taught that way, women feel guilty if they

don't put everybody else's needs first—children, husbands, friends, parents, in-laws, employers, employees. Remember Jan? She was taking care of her four young children, her husband, her gravely ill father, and perhaps a host of other people she didn't even mention. Researchers Luise Eichenbaum and Susie Orbach believe that girls are specifically taught to put their own needs second. Not only do women feel guilty if they don't take care of the needs of others, some even feel guilty if they take care of their own needs!

A corollary to this behavior is that some women have to be sick in order to justify relaxing or taking care of themselves. So, in fact, being sick is the only excuse they have to pay attention to their own needs.

2. *Women have great difficulty saying no to requests for their time or effort.* Girls were taught to camouflage negative feelings. Because it was considered so important to be "nice," girls were told not to be argumentative, oppositional, rejecting or challenging. (Boys, on the other hand, were encouraged to be all of those things.) This one predisposition probably does more to put women's lives out of control than anything else.

3. *Women have difficulty asking for help or delegating tasks.* Many women would rather "do it," whatever "it" is, than ask for help or delegate a task, or pay someone else to do it.

Part of this reluctance to seek help comes from a lifetime of being told not to bother or impose on other people. Some comes also from women's long history of not wanting to hurt someone's feelings by rejecting a request, *and* not wanting to be hurt themselves by having someone reject theirs. Unlike men, women tend to take a no response very personally, which explains why women themselves find it difficult to say no.

4. *Even if women have money, many have great difficulty spending it on themselves.*
"No, I don't have the money."

"No, it's too expensive."

These excuses are standard responses of many women who are reluctant to spend money on healthcare. They'll spend what they have—and more—on their children or other family members. Even among women with high incomes, there is incredible resistance to spending money on themselves, particularly when it's not for health service already covered by an insurance policy. Part of this reluctance reflects the conflicts women feel about giving to themselves. For many women the worst criticism they could hear about themselves was that they were selfish or self-indulgent. Women will do almost anything to avoid feeling selfish or being considered that way by others, even if it means putting off a needed medical examination or not spending money on some worthwhile cultural activity.

5. *Women feel responsible for raising the children and taking care of the household.* Everything in a girl's socialization and training under traditional circumstances was designed around the expectation that someday she would be a mother. While this may be changing, it is still true that 85 percent of all young women expect to have a child some day. From the teenage years through menopause, women deal with child-oriented questions: whether to have a child, with or without a present father; when to have a child, the biological clock that men never worry about; how to rear the child; how to choose child care centers and schools; how to cope with housework; and ways to encourage men to become more involved in parenting, since few men were reared by *their* parents to be fathers. It is taken for granted that if she has a child, a woman will slip into motherhood—naturally, wonderfully, completely. For men, involvement with children is still seen as an optional activity, with kudos given for participation and little criticism if it is not.

Housework is yet another pressure. For most men the home is their haven for rest and relaxation. Not true for women. For them, the home is another workplace—a place where relaxing or resting is out of the question. On a more positive note, however, the household also represents a major source of women's traditional power and control. She carries in her head internalized baggage handed down by her own mother which delineates what should be done, when and by what standards.

Needless to say, little in the socialization process of men prepared them for their homemaker role (except taking out the garbage, repairing broken household objects, heavy lifting and perhaps barbecuing now and then). It is not surprising then that men continue to be only marginally involved with household activities. This alone is a great source of stress for women. In fact, in a recent poll of the Top Ten Stresses, women listed, after "money," "the lack of shared responsibility in the family" as their second highest stress. The household as such didn't even appear on the men's list! As researcher Dolores Curren noted, "This is a stress in itself."[32]

OTHER FACTORS AFFECTING WOMEN

Aside from socialization, there have been certain other factors pressing on the American woman to be who she is and to do what she does. The pressure to work outside the home is among the strongest.

1. *Cultural attitudes.* As noted earlier, more than 60 percent of the women in the United States work outside the home. The most important change since the early '70s has been in cultural values in this very area. While in 1970 there was discernible prejudice against women who "worked," particularly if they had children, today that's reversed: prejudice is shown toward women who don't—even if they have babies!

Recently we have seen somewhat of a backlash movement occurring among some young mothers who prefer to stay home and rear their children. Throughout the country, "mothers at home" are organizing support groups, staging workshops and publishing newsletters to counter against the prevailing "every woman should work" attitude.

2. *Added expectations.* The demands women make upon themselves seem to burgeon almost daily. Encouraged by the media, women find that they must not only dress attractively but they must "dress for success" and in the color of "their season"! It's not enough to cook, let alone cook meals as their mothers did. Today's woman is expected to prepare nutritious and gourmet repasts. It's not enough to have a clean house; today a home must resemble the illustrated pages of a magazine for interior designers. And so the pressures build.

3. *Work environment.* Another major force affecting women is the work environment itself. Management consultants Margaret Hennig and Anne Jardim state that in order for a women to make it in the business world she has to be more competent, more committed, more efficient and more effective than any available man at her current job level, at the job above her, and at the job below.[33] And she still may only get paid a portion of what a man in a comparable role is earning.

In addition, the work world is one created by men, for men, with male values. Most policies and procedures operating in the work world are more reflective of the '50s traditional family than they are of the '80s two-career couple or single-mother families.

WHAT CAN YOU DO?

What do all these changes affecting today's woman mean for you, the health professional? What can you do to help women better meet the stresses and pressures of today's world? How can yours be the healthcare organization that attracts and keeps women as healthcare consumers?

In the past, many healthcare problems distressing to women were casually dismissed.[34] This should no longer happen. You and your organization can do much to see that it doesn't. To begin with, your organization will be effective in meeting women's needs if you first cultivate an institutional attitude which reflects the following messages:

- We understand your special needs.

- We appreciate your pressures, your concerns, your needs.

- We will take your health concerns seriously.

- We can assist you; we are committed to helping you get well or feel better.

This is not an easy task because it requires educating some of your staff. Everyone, from support people to physicians, will need to become cognizant of the societal changes that have shaped contemporary women and appreciate the uniqueness of their needs. Part of this education will be to instill in the healthcare organization a commitment to take women patients seriously by treating *all* complaints as legitimate. Women patients must be made to feel that they have been treated not just competently but with respect.

You will also generate patient patronage if you train your staff to give women permission to take care of themselves. Like Jan, most women come to healthcare organizations feeling ambivalent. If and when they muster the courage to seek treatment, some may feel various degrees of discomfort and self-consciousness in receiving medical attention, even when they are seriously ill. Unless your healthcare professionals assure women of their legitimate right to be treated, their personal sensitivity to receiving care may result in behavior that might actually impede their progress; for example, they might not provide the staff with all relevant information, or they might not follow through with subsequent appointments or maintain accurate medication schedules.

Your organization will be successful in attracting women patients if you address the fundamental issues confronting women today—changing lifestyles, enormous pressures, financial constraints and the difficulty in setting priorities in their lives.

You can demonstrate your organization's sensitivity to women needing healthcare services by offering the following:

- A facility which addresses women's physical, emotional and psychosocial needs, directed by a professional, preferably a woman. At the very least, this director could assemble an up-to-date collection of books, audio cassettes and videotapes focusing on healthcare and mental health issues. She should be knowledgeable about the healthcare organization's resources as well as about community resources that also could assist their women patients. This director should be a model of health (among other things, neither overweight nor overwhelmed).

- Appointments at times and at places convenient to women patients' busy and varied lifestyles.

- Support staff that is courteous, understanding and sympathetic.

- Physicians and nurses who understand the benefits and importance of treating women patients competently and with respect.

- Quality care at affordable prices.

- Attractive facilities.

- Separate hospital quarters with such special amenities as guest trays, a masseuse, beauty services and business services for business women.[35]

- Creation of a behavioral medicine unit to treat stress-related illnesses and emotional problems with behavioral interventions.

- Provision for short-term child care for children while mothers or siblings receive treatment.

You can also demonstrate comprehensiveness by offering programs that meet these women's needs:

- Programs that are reasonably priced, presented at convenient times of the day or night, with parking availability, and announced far enough in advance to allow women time to plan for child care and make other necessary arrangements.

- Programs that offer information about contemporary issues such as stress management, assertiveness training, divorce, balancing family and career, effective delegation techniques, single motherhood, two-career parenting, job success, staying at home with your baby, choosing child care facilities, cultivating great relationships, differences between men and women, communication skills, owning a business, managing personal finances, living a healthy lifestyle, weight control and smoking cessation.

- Special programs for specific target audiences such as women starting their first jobs, new parents, women suffering from stress-related illnesses and women experiencing widowhood.

- Child care offered during the above suggested programs.

Three organizations which stand out in offering the services and programs we have described are: Southwest Florida Regional Medical Center, Ft. Myers, Florida; Humana Hospitals in Phoenix, Arizona, and Aurora, Colorado; Miami Valley Hospital, Dayton, Ohio; and Bethesda Women's Network, Bethesda Hospital, Cincinnati, Ohio.

Finally, it is not enough to simply treat women patients well. Organizations must act consistently. If yours really is serious about meeting women's needs, then it must also recognize the comparable needs of its own women employees. Many healthcare organizations find it difficult to do this; they often don't recognize that it is in their own self-interest to do so.

You might want to urge your organization to consider the following:

1. Be aware of, and respond to, physical and psychological symptoms of overwork and fatigue among female employees. Stage in-service training programs and/or offer counseling to address these problems.

2. Show a willingness to provide a work environment supportive of each employee. Let your employees know you understand that their productivity is dependent upon their physical health and emotional well-being.

3. Provide counseling and in-service training on such topics as stress management, preventive health measures, time management, goal-setting and education in establishing priorities at home and at work.

4. Study precisely who works for your organization, learn about their needs, and consider how—through environmental and/or policy changes—you can elicit greater productivity from them.

5. Be sensitive to the problems of employees who are also parents. Consider providing assistance to them. This can range from in-service programs on how to select child care to day care referral services to on-site child care centers. Few things in an employee's life cause more stress than problems with child care.

6. Examine the organization's current employee options for maternity and paternity leave to care for ill children or elderly parents. You might also want to develop a policy for parents' excused absences to attend important school functions.

7. Consider introducing a flexible work schedule when it is possible and makes sense.

8. Evaluate the prospective availability of responsible, part-time management positions.

Without doubt, healthcare organizations who recognize and respond to their employees' needs gain a competitive edge in the marketplace.

In fact, organizations failing to do so lose good people, increase employee stress levels, experience lower productivity, and are forced to deal with an increasingly negative, dissatisfied work force. Trust that if you respond positively to employee needs and provide them with reasonable options, they, in turn, will be more responsive and productive for you.

NOTES

1. *Statistical Abstract of the United States,* Bureau of the Census, U.S. Department of Commerce, 105th edition, 1985.

2. Hewlett, Sylvia Ann, *A Lesser Life,* New York: William Morrow, 1985, p. 146.

3. Waite, Linda J., "U.S. Women at Work," *Rand,* December, 1981.

4. Hewlett, *A Lesser Life,* p. 98.

5. *Women at Work,* National Commission on Working Women, Spring/ Summer, 1986.

6. "Working Woman: The Myths and Facts," *Los Angeles Herald-Examiner,* November 1, 1983.

7. *Women at Work,* National Commission on Working Women, Spring/ Summer, 1986.

8. Hewlett, *A Lesser Life,* p. 76.

9. *Women at Work,* National Commission on Working Women, Spring/ Summer, 1986.

10. Hewlett, *A Lesser Life,* p. 30.

11. Ibid, p. 344.

12. Ibid, p. 71.

13. Ibid, p. 109.

14. Ibid, p. 71.

15. Ibid, p. 344.

16. Madden, Kathleen, "Success and the Singular Women," *Vogue Magazine*, August, 1986.

17. *Women at Work*, National Commission on Working Women, Spring/Summer, 1986.

18. *Statistical Abstract of the United States*, Bureau of the Census, U.S. Department of Commerce, 105th edition, 1985.

19. Hewlett, *A Lesser Life*, p. 23.

20. *Work and Family; A Changing Dynamic*, The Bureau of National Affairs, Inc., 1986, p. 15.

21. Hewlett, *A Lesser Life*, p. 112.

22. Otten, Allan L., "If You See Families Staging a Comeback, It's Probably a Mirage," *Wall Street Journal*, Sept 25, 1986, p. 1.

23. Hewlett, *A Lesser Life*, p. 5.

24. *Wall Street Journal*, Sept 25, 1986, p. 1.

25. Hewlett, *A Lesser Life*, pp. 65-66.

26. Ibid, p. 89.

27. California Commission on the Status of Women, October, 1983.

28. Ibid, p. 112.

29. Ibid, p. 89.

30. Ibid, p. 80.

31. Ibid, p. 80.

32. Corbett, Ann, "Too Stressed for Sex: The Decline and Fall of Married Love," *The Washington Post*, October 8, 1985, p. B5.

33. Hennig, Margaret and Anne Jardim, *The Managerial Woman*, New York: Pocket Books, 1976.

34. Women's Pavilion, Ft. Meyers Community Hospital, Ft. Myers, Florida.

35. Ibid.

IMPORTANT SEGMENTS AND THEIR IMPLICATIONS

A s we have learned, all women are not alike. The questions that follow from this are, "How are they different?" and "How should these differences affect marketing healthcare services to them?"

The advertising community already knows that successful marketing to women results from clearly defining the significant segments of women in that market.

Northwestern University marketing professor Phillip Kotler describes market segmentation as the task of breaking a total market into segments that share common properties. By segmenting the market, we can arrive at a more finely tuned image of

THERE IS NO TYPICAL BREAST CANCER VICTIM.

IN THE NEXT FIFTEEN MINUTES, THREE WOMEN IN THIS COUNTRY WILL DEVELOP BREAST CANCER

The victim of breast cancer is not always the older woman. Or the woman with a history of breast cancer in her family. Or the woman who "doesn't take care of herself."

The truth is, one in every eleven women will develop breast cancer during her lifetime.

In the time it takes you to study this ad, three more women will have developed the disease.

And one more woman will die from it.

WHY IT'S BETTER TO DETECT BREAST CANCER SOONER THAN LATER

If you're a woman there's only one way to protect yourself against breast cancer: Early detection.

By setting up a monthly routine of Breast Self Examination you can often detect any abnormality leading to breast cancer in its earliest, most curable stages.

Unfortunately, not all forms of breast cancer can be easily discovered in a typical manual exam.

That's why we're asking women past the age of 35 to set up one more lifesaving routine.

An annual visit to the new Diagnostic Breast Center.

INTRODUCING THE DIAGNOSTIC BREAST CENTER AT JFK HOSPITAL

At JFK, we understand how frightening the idea of breast cancer is to a woman. And that's why we're so committed to

our Diagnostic Breast Center. We want to help you live without that fear.

In a simple one-hour visit, you'll be shown a film and given thorough instructions on the lifesaving habit of BSE (Breast Self Examination).

You'll also receive a private, professional examination and a side-low-dose mammogram.

And, depending upon the results of these tests, you'll be introduced to such sophisticated procedures as Transillumination (tight scan) and Ultrasound. New technologies that can diagnose even the

most subtle abnormalities quickly, safely, painlessly.

TAKE LIFE INTO YOUR OWN HANDS CALL US TODAY

You won't need a physician's referral to visit the Diagnostic Breast Center. Simply call 433-3673 for an appointment during our office hours, 8:30 AM to 5 PM, Monday through Friday.

Remember, there is no typical breast cancer victim.

That one woman in eleven looks very much like you.

THE DIAGNOSTIC BREAST CENTER AT JFK HOSPITAL.
150 JFK Circle. Atlantis, Florida 33160
THE FUTURE OF HEALTH CARE IS HERE.

Exhibit 2-1

the woman we're after. In turn, our advertisements will more appropriately match that target woman's concerns and motivation, thus moving her to a favorable purchase decision.

Traditional methods of market segmentation rely heavily on demographic characteristics: age, income, marital status, number of children, etc. At first glance, the JFK Hospital ad (exhibit 2-1), one of a series of three ads with photographs of women ages 35, 45 and 55, seems to reflect marketing to specific age groups. What the series really says, however, is that the hospital recognizes the individuality of women while recognizing that they all are subject to breast cancer.

With the decline of the mass market, this broad brush look is no longer sufficient as a tool, since it fails to evaluate the deeper feelings and values of today's women. To reach these components, additional segmentation techniques are explored. These include: geographic differences and, lately, psychographic and lifestyle variables. Sophisticated marketers have found that all of these categories of analysis play important roles in successfully defining the target female consumer audience. Here's one ad from an institution that recognizes this fact of a woman's life (exhibit 2-2).

TOWARDS A FINER FOCUS ON THE WOMAN

Rena Bartos' book, *The Moving Target*, a landmark in its time, classified women by their values. Subsequently, other studies have been published. One of them with special significance to healthcare is the article, "Marketing Ambulatory Care to Women: A Segmentation Approach," which appeared in the *Journal of Health Care Marketing*, Spring 1985. In their study, authors Professor Gilbert D. Harrell and Matthew F. Fors identify five market segments in the effort to find common values appropriate to women in terms of marketing ambulatory health services. It is an instructive examination of healthcare services in general.

As defined by Harrell and Fors, the five categories are: traditional, family-centered, sports oriented, wellness/wholeness and avoiders.

In terms of their implications for marketing, the family-centered, sports minded and wellness/wholeness segments are the heaviest users of healthcare services. Women in these categories are more experimental, want a lot of information and

PROVIDING HEALTH TO WOMEN THROUGH THE AGES

Good health is so important to a good life. It crosses all boundaries of age and lifestyle. A woman's health is often more biologically complex than that of a man and requires greater understanding and care. The health requirements and needs of women are as individual as women themselves.

At Elliot Hospital our programs are designed to provide healthcare for the whole woman at all

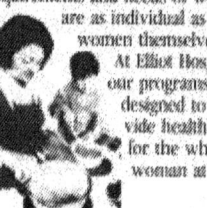

phases of her life. Our commitment to your individual needs has led to such unique programs as the Breast Diagnostic Center and the Infertility Resource Center.

Your need might be for our family and childbirth classes or exercise and nutrition programs.

Our women's health programs speak to the needs of women of all ages and every lifestyle. Each

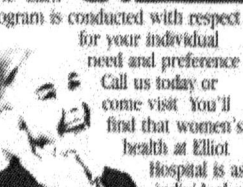

program is conducted with respect for your individual need and preference. Call us today or come visit. You'll find that women's health at Elliot Hospital is as individual as you are.

Women's Health

◼ ELLIOT HOSPITAL

Women's Health • Elliot Hospital • 955 Auburn Street, Manchester, NH 03103 • 603/669-5300

Exhibit 2-2

have a relatively high degree of confidence in making decisions about healthcare.

The authors advise healthcare marketers to identify the segments which exist in their market, then tailor their appeals to these distinct groups through service design, pricing, marketing communication and points of distribution.

Harrell and Fors' five categories serve as a highly useful start in classifying segments of women in your target marketplace. As a practical application, the following Case Study (exhibit 2-3) demonstrates how the characteristics of these target audiences are translated, first into the creative concept and then the tangible product—a direct mail piece.

Case Study: A Diagnostic Breast Health Center

Background: The Diagnostic Breast Medical Group opened in a suburb of greater Los Angeles. Available research showed that the women in this population were conservative and primarily pink collar or new collar workers. Generally, they held administrative or clerical positions, mainly in support capacities. They owned homes, were married and had families. The community was stable, family-oriented and traditional.

Analysis: We believed that a family-centered, traditional market would be difficult to persuade to utilize a health service in a traditional way.

We also knew, through research, that the community's typical woman, (i.e., the mother) was oriented to providing the guidance and nurturing to her family, while neglecting her own healthcare needs.

With the exception of an annual visit to her gynecologist for a Pap smear, and a growing acceptance and participation in aerobics exercise programs, these women typically would postpone or ignore their own physical problems.

Creative Rationale: With the fitness trend sweeping the coun-

Exhibit 2-3

try, women were spending more time in aerobic classes and on running tracks, buying Jane Fonda workout tapes and selecting high fiber cereals from the grocery shelves. Prompted by features on television and in women's magazines on the benefits of fitness, increasing numbers of women were questioning traditional medicine's practices (for example, visit your physician only when you're desperately ill, etc.).

The headline, "Taking Charge of Your Health is Taking Charge of Your Life," capitalized on this fitness trend and suggested the appropriateness of seeking healthcare services outside of traditional physician channels. In fact, it was more than acceptable—it was a strong, positive statement of approval for self-referral to the DMBG.

The visual in the advertisement, a group of women of all ages and ethnic backgrounds, helped individual women identify with the message. Dressed in leotards, the women in the illustration underscored today's concern for fitness.

The strategy of the ad's copy centered on the issues of family, the importance of taking care of oneself, and the caution that breast screening, like the Pap smear, was an important health maintenance regimen for women. A list of typical objections served to remove the problem of resistance from the purely technical diagnostic procedure and state it in more familiar terms. In approaching this segment of the market psychologically, the copy emphasizes the software—not the hardware—of the problem, and helps break down resistance to utilizing this service. Even the issue of low dosage radiation was discussed as a benefit rather than a technological issue.

ANOTHER WAY OF SEEING OUR MARKET

Other ways of seeing segments of women amplify and extend our vision. Rather than a definitive classification, these categories demonstrate the diverse ways marketers must look at women.

The Unfulfilled/The Lonely/The Frustrated

A woman who might be successful in her career may also be a heavy drinker. Alcoholic beverage purchases and consumption by women is increasing. The working mother, juggling many responsibilities in her life, might be dabbling in drugs to help her juggle even better. Marijuana to mellow-out, cocaine to pep-up, Valium to sleep and anti-depressives to counteract those lows—all are too readily available as mother's helpers. Food is also a drug for certain women and the gamut of eating disorders—obesity, anorexia, bulimia—are symptoms of deep-seated problems.

One of the growing health problems for today's women is fatigue. Health professionals are realizing that fatigue creates a variety of problems that have nothing to do with the amount of sleep women get but everything to do with their levels of personal satisfaction.

Fatigue-ridden women often fill the gaps in their lives with destructive behavior—substance abuse (see Case Study, exhibit 2-4), eating disorders, parenting problems. These women can be reached with comprehensive treatment programs that include nutrition, counseling, medical intervention and behavioral clinics and seminars.

Case Study: Century City Hospital's Drugs Ad

Century City Hospital is situated among affluent Los Angeles communities. Beverly Hills, Century City, Hollywood are all areas where lifestyles are luxurious, fast-tracked, high-pressured and, for the women, oftentimes lonely. For this population of middle-aged women married to highly successful men, the pressures to drink and take drugs are very high. In identifying these women as a specific market segment we wish to capture, an ad was created using a woman who clearly represented our target segment of this population. Attractively dressed, wearing good jewelry and with well-coiffed hair and obviously manicured nails, but a very sad demeanor, she epitomized the visual we wanted.

The copy supported the fact that many times women turn to medications or, even worse, illegal drugs, to generate a sense of well-being they may not be enjoying when they're sober. The ad copy tries to be realistic in suggesting why they choose to abuse themselves. At the same time, it is slanted to make them realize that there are compelling reasons to turn to a different lifestyle.

When addressing this population, it helps to lay the responsibility for their behavior on them. An affluent population is typically a controlling, in-charge group seldom willing to relinquish responsibility. Therefore, the emphasis in the ads was on "You gotta wanna beat 'em" or "You've got to take charge and make the decision."

It's also effective to offer them solutions and rewards to reinforce their progress with recognition. Establish "success

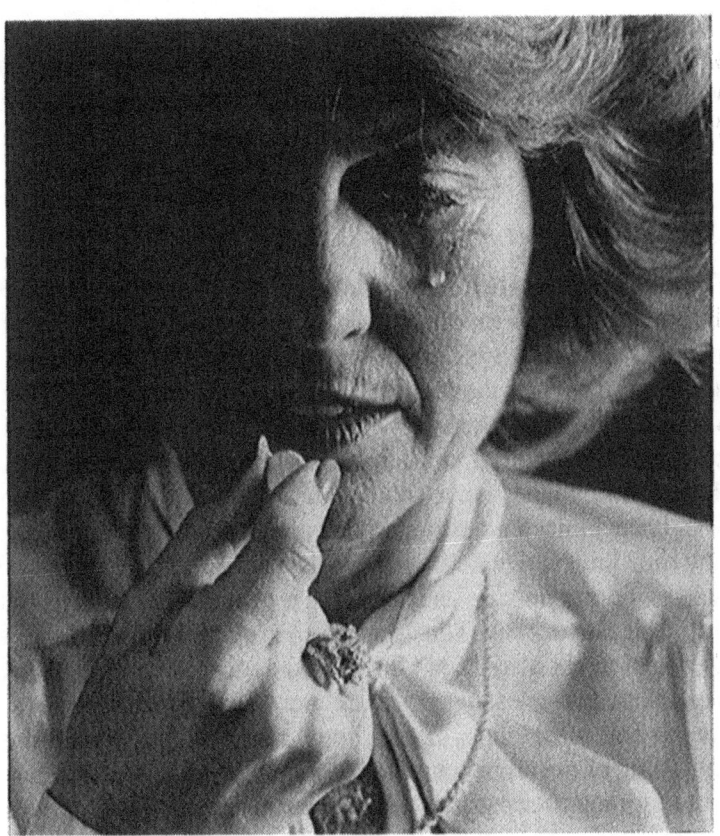

DRUGS
YA GOTTA WANNA BEAT 'EM.

It starts simply enough
A crisis here, a crisis there
And before you know it, you're
dependent on getting high,
coming down, being mellow or
just not feeling anything at all

Maybe that's your goal — to
not feel But then again, maybe
it isn't And if it really isn't, we
can help

**ISN'T THERE SOMETHING
MORE IMPORTANT
TO LIVE FOR THAN DRUGS?**

Century City Hospital
2070 Century Park East
Los Angeles, CA 90067
(213) 277-4248
Fran Roa, Director

ALCOHOLISM
UNIT

Exhibit 2-4

clubs," where reaching certain goals is the price of admission. Membership allows them to square their new selves with other women who have overcome comparable personal obstacles. (See Case Study, exhibit 2-5.)

Case Study: College Hospital Cathy Rigby Ad

The challenge was to create an ad that would be attention getting and sensitive to the needs of women who suffer from bulimia. Using Cathy Rigby, who is a bulimic, as a spokesperson was an added advantage. Her story emphasized how women who are obsessed with their weight also become obsessed with their appearance to an unnatural extent. They distort their ability to see themselves realistically, and, therefore, have a misconception, an out-of-focus orientation about how they look and who they are. Our marketing goal in this ad was to communicate that message visually as well as to emphasize it verbally. The creative strategy we selected was a photograph of Cathy Rigby in varying degrees of focus and/or happiness, pro-gressing from the most out-of-focus perspective to the most clear, happy appearance of her. From the beginning of the ad, where the copy states that you don't have to be famous to focus on your appearance, to its end, where we emphasize that you'll like what you see, the reader is carried through the problem to the solution in a combination of strong verbal and visual impact.

The Cathy Rigby print ad has enjoyed tremendous success for College Hospital, amounting to a large number of calls and subsequent admissions as a result of it.

Many problems beleaguering women may be work-related, creating inordinate stress, and may be reached through an Employee Assistance Program, in cooperation with local employers.

"You don't have to be famous to focus on your figure."

"Though thousands of women do. Yet for so many, that focus gets distorted so that every pound becomes magnified. Which can lead to dangerous behavior. Self starvation, the binge/purge cycle of bulimia and compulsive overeating are major problems.

Like so many women, I got caught in a binge/purge cycle that seemed out of control.

But I found a way to regain control and you can, too. With treatment plans like The College Program from caring professionals who work with you, not on you, to help you get your life back into focus.

If you or someone you know has an eating disorder call The College Program, available at College Hospital.

You'll like what you see."

Cathy Rigby

College Hospital
Working Together to Get You Better
1-800-352-3301
Most insurance plans accepted

Exhibit 2-5

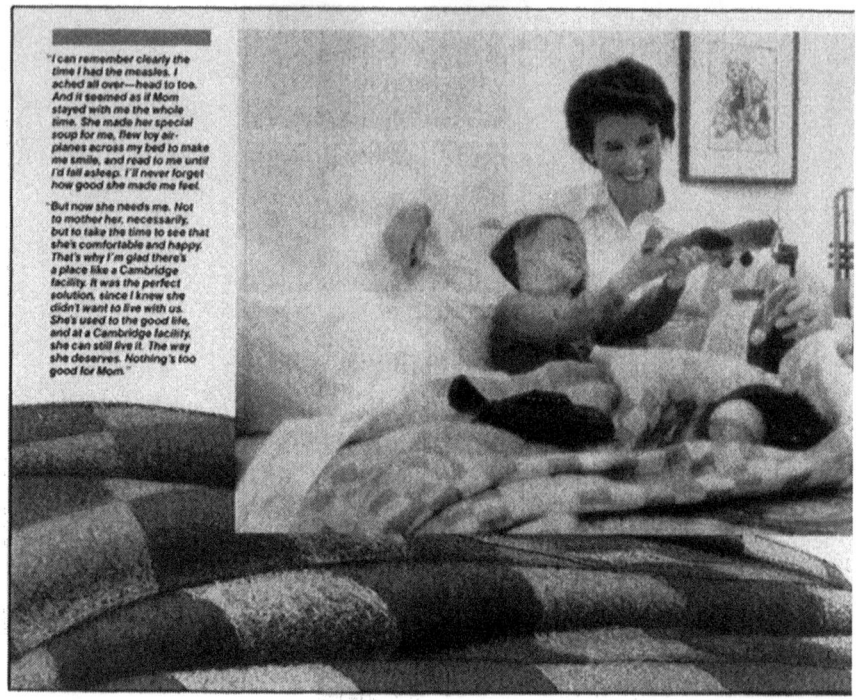

"I can remember clearly the time I had the measles. I ached all over—head to toe. And it seemed as if Mom stayed with me the whole time. She made her special soup for me, flew toy airplanes across my bed to make me smile, and read to me until I'd fall asleep. I'll never forget how good she made me feel.

"But now she needs me. Not to mother her, necessarily, but to take the time to see that she's comfortable and happy. That's why I'm glad there's a place like a Cambridge facility. It was the perfect solution, since I knew she didn't want to live with us. She's used to the good life, and at a Cambridge facility, she can still live it. The way she deserves. Nothing's too good for Mom."

Exhibit 2-6

The Active Mature

This middle-aged woman belongs to the Sandwich Generation—caught between the demands of teenage or young adult children and her aging parents or in-laws. Free from the financial burdens of children but possibly faced with the emotional responsibility for an elderly, infirm mother and/or father, the active mature woman also has to deal with the conflict arising from enjoying some of the indulgences she previously postponed and the self-conscious concern that perhaps she is being selfish.

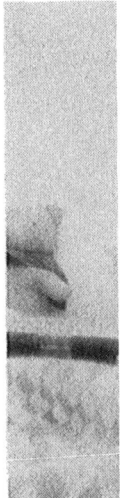

THE CARING CONTINUES...

Above all else, we strive to provide our residents with thoughtful, compassionate care. The same kind of care they have given to their loved ones all the years of their lives.

When appropriate, before new residents move to our facilities, they are visited by Cambridge staff members. These informal visits make it possible for new residents and their families to feel comfortable with the staff and to gain a better understanding of the Cambridge lifestyle. In turn, our acquaintance with the residents' families enables us to better meet their individual needs. In addition, all admissions personnel are health care professionals, ensuring residents of an accurate medical assessment prior to their admission.

Each of our campuses have a major hospital located nearby. And, each campus has facilities which provide a continuum of health care, dedicated to meeting our residents' present and future medical needs.

A team of medical specialists, including physical therapists, speech therapists, staff physicians and laboratory and pharmaceutical personnel, are involved in the care of each patient. An on-staff dietician plans special, therapeutic diets. And, full time social workers and therapeutic recreational therapists play vital roles in our health care program, as well. We do of course encourage our residents' private physicians to direct and monitor their care.

At the heart of the Cambridge health care program is our outstanding staff of Registered Nurses, on duty 24 hours a day, providing the special concern and attention so necessary for recuperation and the maintenance of a positive mental attitude.

If she has living parents, this woman has to face the decision of long-term residential care versus bringing the parent into her home. Whether daughter or daughter-in-law, the primary decision often rests with her. She has to overcome an enormous guilt that prevents her from making these decisions with anything but a heavy heart unless she can be convinced she is doing the right thing, choosing the right option. (See Case Study, exhibit 2-6.)

Case Study: Cambridge Nursing Home Brochure

Background: Cambridge Group, Inc., is a company which

owned and operated private long-term care nursing homes in the East and Midwest. They targeted their marketing efforts to affluent adults—children of the elderly—as well as physicians, planners aiding discharged patients, lawyers and estate planners. However, the group's primary target was the adult daughter (or daughter-in-law). The central obstacle in dealing with nursing home admittance for a loved one is the sense of failure in not being able to care for the parent at home (for whatever reason) and the overwhelming guilt in opting to send him or her to a nursing home.

Creative Rationale: At the onset, the negative image of a nursing home had to be confronted. The luxury of the Cambridge homes helped to reduce that concern, but it still existed.

By introducing nostalgia, we were able to help potential prospects identify with the message and simultaneously reduce some of the misconceptions about nursing home care. The "remember when you were helpless/vulnerable and mom or dad cared for you" theme moved the reader to the logical conclusion: it's comforting to know that there's a place like Cambridge to care for their parent in a manner consistent with what they deserved.

The visuals—tinted photographs—evoked distant but treasured times and places.

The copy approach is twofold. One story line deals with how things used to be, the other with how things are now in terms of the benefits associated with this chain of nursing homes. The benefits provided reassurance to the family.

Note: Interestingly, men considered the brochure too emotional and heart-rending. They were more interested in the "hardware": the living arrangements, number of meals, types of medical services provided, etc. Women reacted quite differently; they were emotionally touched and moved by the copy. They related strongly to it, warmed by the accoutrements, companionship and recreational opportunities their parents would enjoy. For them, the "software" emphasis was

A Day For Children Who Care For Parents.

Sooner or later, every family is faced with the care for an aging parent. And that can put stress on the strongest family.

If you care for an aging parent now, or see that possibility in your family's future, we can help.

This Saturday is a free, day long seminar that can guide you through the legal, financial, medical and emotional problems you'll encounter when caring for an aging parent.

You'll hear speakers from the hospital staff and other experts in the field. You'll see exhibits from home care providers and support groups.

You can spend the entire day, or part of the day, learning how to take care of a parent and still take care of yourself.

To register, call 320-3911, ext. 486. This is a free seminar no child can afford to miss.

Options for the Aging (9 - 10:30 a.m.)
Financial Concerns (10:45- 11:45 a.m.)
Lunch and Exhibits (11:45- 1 p.m.)
Legal Issues (1- 2 p.m.), or
Caring For The Homebound (1- 2 p.m.)
Emotional Issues For The Caregiver (2:15 - 3:15 p.m.)

Chippenham Hospital

Chippenham Parkway and Jahnke Road Richmond, Virginia 23225

Caring For Your Aging Parent. A Free Seminar At Chippenham Hospital, October 26.

Exhibit 2-7

on target. Other options are seen in the MedCenters Health Plan and Chippenham Hospital ads (exhibits 2-7 and 2-8). Other characteristics of the active mature woman provide additional marketing opportunities. With the income to satisfy her needs, and with an interest in health maintenance and self-improvement, such areas as plastic surgery, cardiac and general fitness, nutrition, behavior and lifestyle become important health issues. With her children's college education and the mortgage paid (or provided for), she is financially comfortable enough to ask "*Where* are the best doctors?" for herself and her husband. The Century Pavilion ad (exhibit 2-9) appealed to the upscale segment of this group, along with others who desired the privacy and luxury the unit afforded.

The Active Elderly

Qualitatively different than the active mature, the active elderly is one of the fastest growing age categories in America.

We're Doing Everything We Can To Keep Seniors In Their Place.

At MedCenters Health Plan we know you didn't spend a lifetime making a home, only to have health problems force you out of it.

So our MedCenters MediCare program is designed to help you keep your independence Not just with complete HMO coverage, but with special senior benefits suggested by our Senior Advisory Board

For example, we offer classes on hypertension And weight loss And osteoporosis And sleeping disorders Even sexuality.

We also offer a comprehensive dental plan and 43 neighborhood locations, including Park Nicollet Medical Center.

When it's prescribed by your doctor, we provide home nursing care So if you do get sick, chances are very good that you can recover in your own home. Where you'll be most comfortable

We even have a Division of Geriatric Medicine and Health that's entirely devoted to research and programs that will make sure nothing comes between you and your independence in the future

To get the whole story about MedCenters MediCare, call 927-3995 (Outside the Twin Cities, call toll free 1-800-642-0091) Or mail the coupon

Then sit back and put your feet up

Because if we have anything to say about it, you're going to stay right where you are for a good, long time

---

For more information, call 927-3995.
(Outside the Twin Cities, call 1-800-642-0091 toll free)

Or mail coupon to: MedCenters Health Plan,
4951 Excelsior Boulevard St. Louis Park MN 55416

☐ *I'd like to know more about MedCenters MediCare*

Name _____

Address _____

City _____

State _____ Zip _____

Phone ( ) _____

MEDCENTERS HEALTH PLAN

43 locations including ✪ Park Nicollet Medical Center

Exhibit 2-8

Dr. Leonard Swartzman, a Los Angeles physician specializing in gerontology, described this generation as experiencing "the season of loss": loss of spouse, money, health, friends, power and hair. For many, these collective losses lead to lonely and frustrating years.

Although medical science has enabled the active elderly to extend their lives, they nonetheless frequently experience chronic disabilities: their eyes dim, their hands falter, their walk slows. Yet many are still able to maintain independent lives and enjoy attending educational, social and cultural activities.

Healthcare organizations often target this group with outreach programs on pertinent health issues related to the elderly. For example, Century City Hospital in Los Angeles presents a monthly lecture series for senior citizens in conjunction with a local community center. The hospital's doctors volunteer their time to discuss depression, drugs, alcoholism, sexual dysfunction, foot care and many other pertinent topics. The hospital underpins the series by distributing promotional information. Each lecture draws at least 200 attendees; often several in the audience will ask the guest-speaking doctors for their business cards.

What this program does, like other comparable lecture series around the country, is establish a link with the hospital that these senior adults appreciate. By acquainting senior adult women with the hospital's facility and personnel, they also generate a loyalty which will be exercised when they make decisions about impending healthcare needs. Since she's still active, the healthcare decision will be hers, not her daughter's or daughter-in-law's . . . yet. The Queen of the Valley Hospital ad (exhibit 2-10) illustrates one such approach.

Some marketing programs employ other components. A hot meal offered at a special discount and served in the hospital's dining facility during off-peak hours is one such attraction. A concert, movie or discussion group are others.

Exhibit 2-9

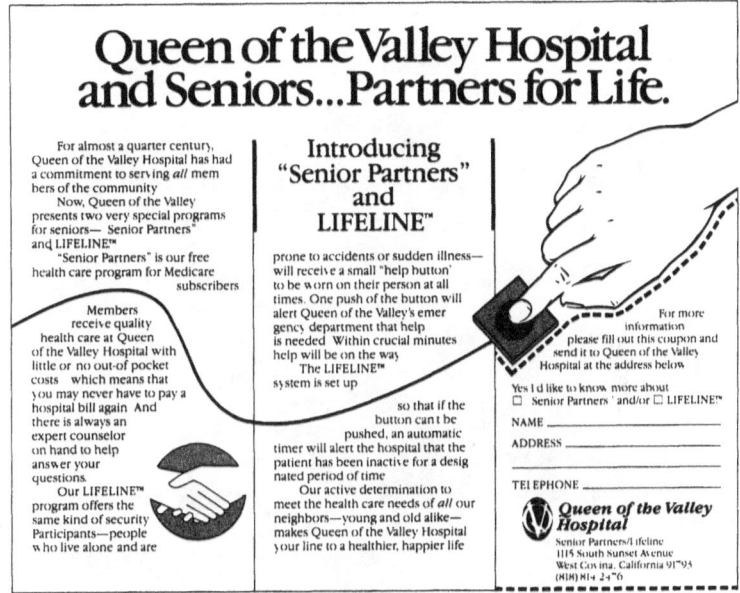

Exhibit 2-10

The thrust of these programs is to enhance the personal connection and comfort level of the senior woman to the facility and its staff.

The Working Mother

The most talked about category in terms of its sheer rate of growth and significant size, the working mother is a major segment of many hospital market areas.

Not only are women getting into the work force earlier, but if they drop out for a period to have children, they re-enter it very quickly. Over 52 percent of women are now in the work force, and fully 35 percent of them are working mothers with children under six years of age.

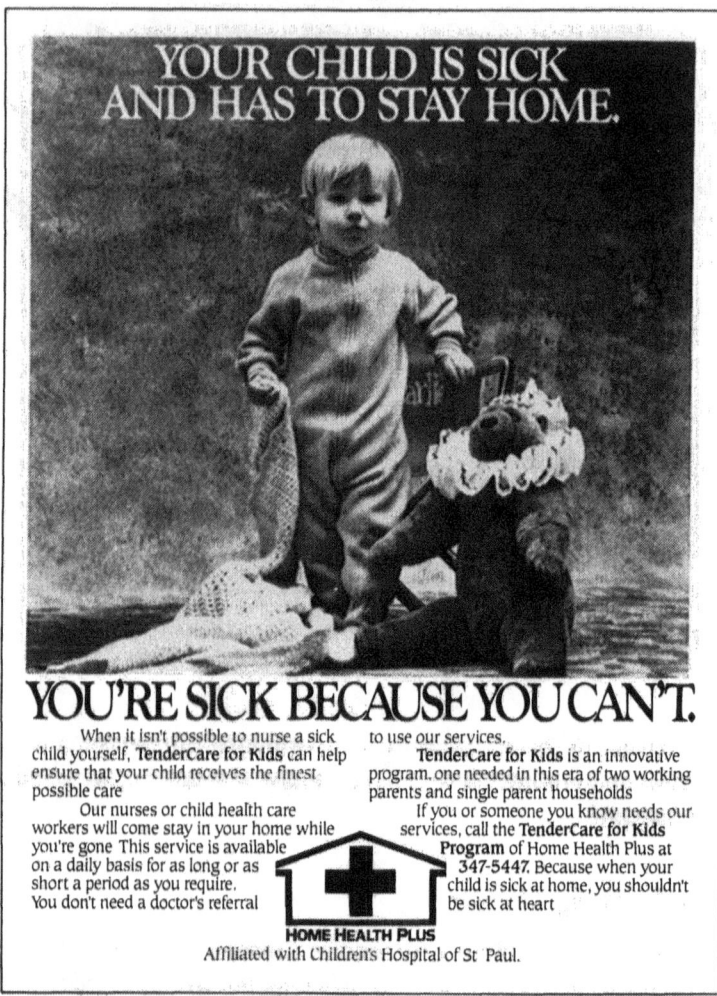

Exhibit 2-11

This impressive and increasing number of working mothers presents several important marketing opportunities for healthcare providers. Urgent Care facilities are one service that have emerged to satisfy the demand for more convenient accesses to healthcare. Extended hours, express service, babysitter hotlines and day care for mildly ill children are appreciated and supported by this group. Torn between the demands of her job and the healthcare needs of her young children, the working mother readily utilizes understanding and supportive help for herself and her family when it is made available. The Home Health Care Plus ad (exhibit 2-11) clearly demonstrates the point: your child is sick, and has to stay home. This sensitive ad addresses the key concerns of the parent. The copy explains benefits to the consumer without boring the reader with "hardware" information such as how many nurses the facility has on staff or how many years the institution has been in business.

The Yuppie Mom

The Yuppie Mom perhaps represents one of the most significant categories to target since she is a most discerning consumer of everything, including healthcare. This woman typically enjoys a greater income and the lifestyle it affords. Travel may have been, or is still, commonplace for her and, as a result, she is sophisticated, having stayed at better hotels, eaten at nicer restaurants and enjoyed a high level of service.

The Yuppie Mom is used to making decisions and managing professional issues, and therefore she evaluates those products and services that affect her or her family with an even greater critical eye than her non-Yuppie counterpart. Used to being efficient and decisive, she responds to information, attitudes and a service orientation.

You generally will not find this woman patiently cooling her heels in a doctor's office or rushing to fill prescriptions for drugs she knows nothing about. She will be the patient who will expect a little more time in order to get sufficient information from the medical establishment. She will discuss articles and data she has gathered on her own about a medical problem.

Everything's normal with their baby. They're sure of it. But Sally and Tom have asked their doctor to schedule delivery at Mount Sinai. Just in case.

Of course, there's a full range of birthing options and family centered care. But of more importance: no hospital in the state offers such comprehensive obstetric programs.

Our programs begin even before pregnancy. Mount Sinai offers a full range of fertility services, including one of the few in vitro fertilization centers in the state.

Mount Sinai's early care specialists and programs can identify problems before they become problems. Genetics counseling. Ultrasound. Amniocentesis. We work to keep diabetes or other chronic disease from complicating pregnancy. We help turn high risk pregnancies into low risk ones. With this kind of preventive care, our cesarean rate is the lowest in the city.

Our genetics lab, the only full service facility like it in southeastern Wisconsin, helps you understand the risks and the choices in your reproductive life. If a family member has a genetic disorder. If you've had several miscarriages. Or if you're over 35 and contemplating pregnancy.

Even though everything is smooth and normal with your pregnancy, our doctors know to expect the unexpected. At Mount Sinai, we have a Neonatal Intensive Care Unit that gives babies as small as 1½ pounds a fighting chance at life. And physicians who are specialists in the unique problems of the newborn.

Sally and Tom have worked incredibly hard to feel secure enough to have their first baby. They're not going to take any chances. They're playing it safe at the most secure hospital they can find.

For complete information on any of our services, please call 289-8009.

MILWAUKEE'S WORLD-CLASS HOSPITAL

MOUNT SINAI MEDICAL CENTER
950 North 12th Street

Exhibit 2-12

She will investigate the most qualified pediatrician with the zeal of a reporter, seeking recommendations, references and medical credentials. She wants quality in her life and will spend more to get it. Budget floor medicine would not appeal to this woman. In fact, the opposite may be true.

Today's Yuppie Mom wants the best for her children. You see her interest in fashion, toys and enrichment classes for them. Anything that can help her assist her child in getting a competitive edge in the world, the Yuppie Mom will pursue. Nothing but the best for her child!

The Yuppie Woman's attitude, it should be noted, is not solely related to income. It is an outgrowth of enlightened consciousness, arising out of years of consumerism, feminism and education and all leading to higher expectations for quality products and services. Consider the ad for Mount Sinai Medical Center in Milwaukee (exhibit 2-12).

First of all, it takes a worldly person to know what standard "world class" represents. This ad is targeted specifically to the Yuppie Mom who is accustomed to quality on a grand scale. The copy reads, "Sally and Tom have worked incredibly hard to feel secure enough to have their first baby. They're not going to take any chances. They're playing it safe at the most secure hospital they can find."

The copy emphasizes the quality of services at Mount Sinai, acknowledges that both parents work and shows an understanding why they aren't going to skimp on quality at this important time.

While other segments of the female populace may follow, this Yuppie category sets the trends and standards that others will grow to expect in the provision of healthcare.

The Ethnic Woman

Ethnicity introduces still another dimension to the woman that must be respected in developing any effective marketing program. And the approach chosen depends on the particular ethnic group. In general, though, the woman in all ethnic groups is the backbone of the family, aspiring each member to do better. She, like her Yuppie compatriot, will not tolerate second rate medicine. Therefore, marketers must instill a feeling of confidence that quality care is available to her and her family as respected individuals, as part of the community and not singled out as members of a minority.

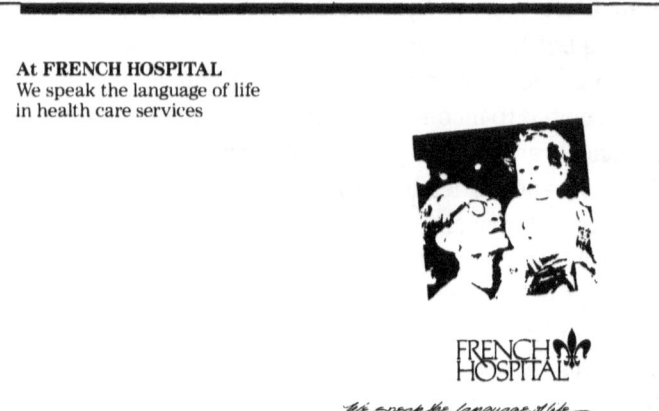

At **FRENCH HOSPITAL**
We speak the language of life
in health care services

Exhibit 2-13

Note how the French Hospital in Los Angeles (exhibit 2-13) solved the problem of marketing to its multi-ethnic community with quality materials and a first-class approach. While recognizing and respecting the many languages and cultures of its community, the headline represents an implicit acceptance of the individuality of the ethnic group while "mainstreaming" it as part of American life. Acceptance is a cherished value of immigrant groups, even though they want to hold on to their traditional identities.

In marketing to ethnic groups, it is important to know, for example, that Hispanic women are not homogeneous. New immigrants from Mexico are different from second and third generation Mexican-Americans, who, in turn, vary from Cubans, Guatemalans and El Salvadorans. Each is distinctive in language, dialect, customs and traditions.

In general, continuity of family relationships is of paramount importance to this population. They are exceedingly brand loyal (some say this is because they are most familiar with those American brands marketed in their country of origin) and respond favorably to any reinforcement of their cultures. However, those who assimilate fast are drawn to American products. Hispanic women are culturally traditional, tend to stay close to home and yield to the man of the family as the primary decision-maker.

However, in terms of decisions about healthcare, Hispanic women wield considerable influence. But, because some still have difficulty with English as a second language, they tend to be most receptive to healthcare information that is telecast or broadcast or displayed on outdoor advertising, preferably in their native language. In some markets, Spanish language television and newspapers are their primary source of information. A highly effective way to reach this population is through their children. Visits by healthcare representatives to schools, tours of a healthcare facility and easy-to-read informational leaflets are good reinforcers and will appeal to Hispanic women.

Black women are often reached in consumer advertising in generic black advertising campaigns, regardless of the product. And the more affluent the black women's audience, the more the tone seems to take on a white coloration. "In talking to marketers, I have found that people often assume the richer a black person gets, the whiter she gets," observes Sara Burroughs, Senior Vice President and General Manager of Burrell Advertising in Chicago. Certainly, the challenge of segmentation within this market is equally as important as in any other female population group. However, those black women aspiring to upward mobility tend to buy higher priced and higher status products, although their income may skew them demographically, according to Lafette Jones, President of Smith, Jones and Associates.

Black women between the ages of 25-35 represent the most intensive population of working women, higher than any other segment of this general category. They are keenly concerned with service and value, and they want to make sure they are getting the best of both.

An Oriental woman, on the other hand, has her own set of concerns. The hardest group to reach through market research, she places high value on a healthcare provider's credentials and technology. Often, she has experienced a different form of health care as part of her culture and, as a result, is less influenced or impressed by the American system. Hospital staff and physicians who speak her language have a decided advantage over those who do not, since it helps to bridge the gap between the cultures.

Oriental women also are not a homogeneous group. Unresolved historical issues and language and cultural differences exist between the Chinese, Japanese, Koreans and other oriental groups. When marketing to this population or other foreign groups, astute marketers must be sensitive to these differences and take extreme caution in producing informational and promotional materials that are appropriate in every sense. Knowledgeable translators and typesetters are valuable resources for anyone marketing to an ethnic population, but do not rely on them totally. Verify all text for your target foreign market for cultural/semantic nuances.

For the California Hospital in Los Angeles, the challenge in reaching the oriental market—to alert them to a price discount if they'd pay cash in advance for the hospital's delivery of a baby—was to find a universal symbol that was acceptable and readily understandable in order to capture their attention. The outlined baby bottle satisfied this need, and the information was basically straightforward. Visually, note the avoidance of any form of emotional appeal, and any stereotyped messages, in their ad (exhibit 2-14).

Exhibit 2-14

The Young Woman: Single/Married/With or Without Career

We once conducted a series of focus groups with women of varying ages to assess their level of interest in utilizing health facilities run for and by women. The three age categories included women ages 18-25, 26-40 and 41-55. Of all the groups, the youngest was the least receptive to the concept. Their experience with the medical establishment was limited to their childhood family doctor, a family planning clinic at their college or, in some cases, a gynecologist for the purpose of obtaining birth control pills. Few had experience with childbirth or, for that matter, with any serious illness.

The attitudes of these young women, in general, were simple: they felt more comfortable with male physicians since they still considered men more authoritative and competent. In some cases, these women were actually uncomfortable with the idea of another woman examining them because it conjured up threats of lesbianism.

Important to this category, however, were issues of cost. For most of these young ladies, the concern over health insurance and out-of-pocket expenses was new. The reality of the financial burden of their own healthcare makes them most receptive to the advantages of prepaid health plans.

This younger segment of the women's population is still very much influenced by their parents' choices and recommendations of healthcare services. The way to get their attention is to focus on those problems relevant to them. Sexually transmitted diseases, fitness, nutrition, finances, birth control or the decision to have children are some of the helpful topics that could encourage young women to establish a relationship with a facility or provider.

Segments Within Segments

Any general categorization of the total woman population naturally creates gaps and questions since we know some women who cross into several segments simultaneously—or who defy any type of segmentation.

A working mother with children under the age of six faces different healthcare problems than one whose children are grown. A career woman is different from the woman working just part-time to earn enough to buy new living room furniture.

The challenge, therefore, is to select the exact motivators that will influence your audience to act or react the way you want it to. While you can never sell a woman something she doesn't want, you can tailor your message in such a way that, when she is in the market to buy what you are selling, she will buy from you.

COMMON MYTHS

To summarize, the obvious mistake in marketing to women is to think of the market as one uniform group of females. And by now we know better. But let's examine some commonly held myths that might still color our perception of the women's market and use it as a first step toward arriving at a better understanding of who we are talking to.

"All Women Are Like the Women We Know"

It's easy to think of our female customers as similar to our wives, sisters, daughters, mothers, grandmothers, friends and associates. But the women you know don't necessarily have the same responses or concerns as the ones you hope will call or come into your healthcare organization. Marketing strictly by the numbers can't be done any more. Women defy segmentation by age, income, career, status, children, etc. A single working mother will respond differently than a married working mother. Working mothers with teenaged children have different concerns than working mothers with children under six. It makes a difference whether she's married or single, widowed or divorced. And the women you know may be unlike any in your target audience.

"Ethnic Women Are All Alike"

Not so. Chinese women respond to credentials and authority; black women to service; Hispanic women to quality brand names. Adding specific ethnicity to a woman further defines her, giving an extra measure of depth to her already complex nature.

"All Women Are Alike"

How about lonely women? Successful ones? Those who are wealthy? Mothers? Farmers versus urban women? Young adult women just starting their careers versus empty nesters?

"If All Women Aren't Alike, Then We Can't Reach Them"

As we'll see in the next chapter, reaching such a vast and immensely diverse audience can be accomplished by addressing those universal qualities intrinsic to the woman's experience today.

Some Not So Common, Common Denominators

I n the real world, many different types of women appear in a healthcare organization's demographic and psychographic profile. A typical market area will contain segments of mothers, working women and what we have identified as the active mature, among others. A healthcare organization's program or service, such as substance abuse, may be appropriate for several of these market segments. With so many differences revealed among women, the marketer's task to advertise and promote one program is formidable indeed. How do we reach and motivate a cross-section of women?

Marketers can be led astray by focusing too

closely on women's differences. Successful marketing commu-
nications must appeal to the underlying, basic issues that
concern *all* women. For, regardless of their age, marital status,
number of children, education and the countless other variables that exist, certain common denominators characterize
today's women. By tapping into these common concerns, marketers will be able to appeal to the broadest potential base
possible in advertising and promoting a healthcare product or
service without losing their target woman in the process.

Thus, no matter how one chooses to classify the complex
variety of today's women, appealing to these commonalities
promotes efficient marketing.

COMMON DENOMINATORS OF WOMEN

1. *Women desire to be treated with respect and empathy.* By
their sheer numbers and purchasing power, women have
become a vital force in the marketplace. Since the 1960s in
particular, the consciousness of women in general has risen to
such an extent that it has created an environment wherein
women feel a need to be educated, successful, productive and
valued. Whatever the actual reality of their respective lives,
women like to be addressed with the assumption they have
those qualities.

Accommodating this need may be as simple and direct as
addressing her correctly and respectfully. Sensitive physicians, for example, are careful to address their female patients
as Miss, Mrs. or Ms. and other appropriate titles in personal
contact or written correspondence, rather than by using first
names.

Or it may be as subtle as the tone, as in the ads for the
Breast Health Center of Children's Hospital of San Francisco
(exhibit 3-1) and the Redondo Beach Medical Group (exhibit
3-2).

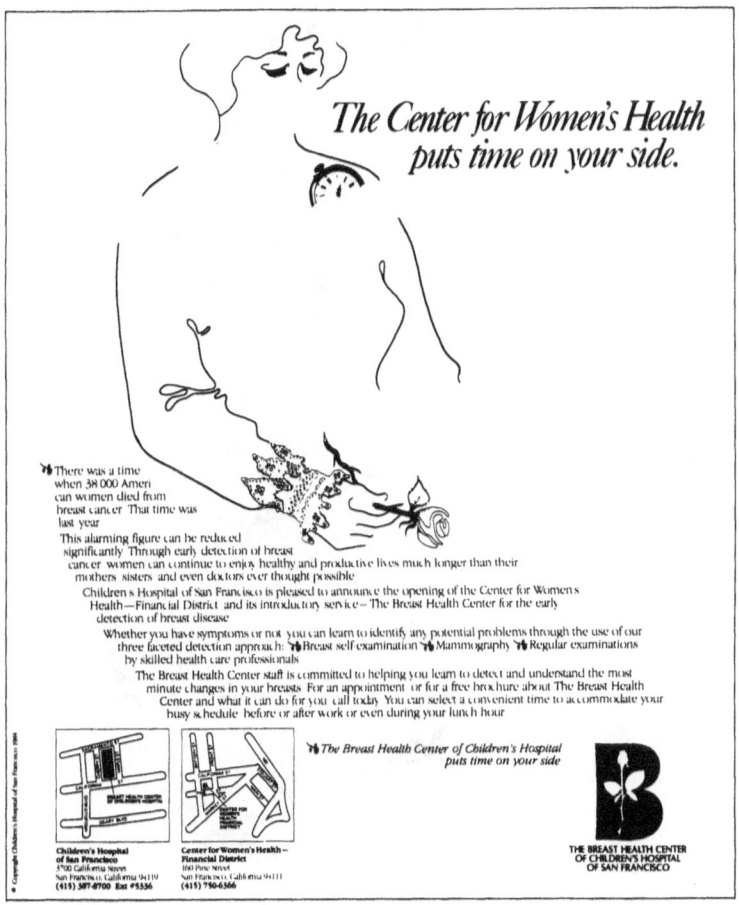

Exhibit 3-1

Today's woman wants to be talked to, not talked down to. She understands that while the medical establishment may not have all the answers, she wants it recognized that she is capable of understanding the answers she is given in response to her questions.

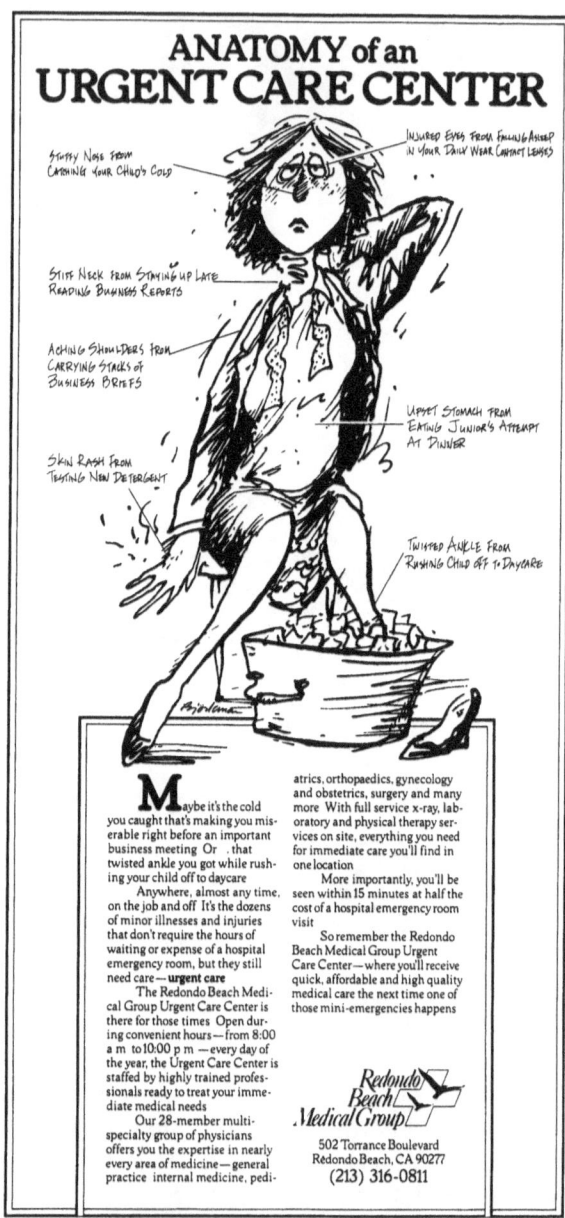

Exhibit 3-2

2. *Women value their time.* Despite all the electronic home appliances available to simplify her domestic chores, today's woman enjoys 30 percent less leisure time now than her counterpart ten years ago. In addition to satisfying her traditional roles of wife, mother, daughter and friend, she must also confront the increased demands on her to be educated, healthy, interesting, beautiful, productive and financially secure. In truth, today's woman is trying to do more to attain a successful life than her time permits.

Healthcare services are often guilty of ignoring a woman's race against time. A woman who has made a medical appointment—and rearranged her schedule at considerable inconvenience to do so—can only do a slow, resentful burn if delayed too long in the waiting room. Of course, women do understand that emergencies can arise. But when they do, a woman wishes to be notified, ahead of time if possible. A thoughtful recognition that her time is indeed valuable and some suggestion that meanwhile others are trying to accommodate her would prove most salutary in such a situation.

Unfortunately, much of healthcare today is still organized around the doctor's schedule or the hospital's convenience—rather than the consumer. For example, early morning, dinner hour and Saturday appointments are relatively rare. With competition increasing, however, the perceptive marketer will seize the opportunity to capture a segment of the female population by introducing off-conventional hours services.

Healthcare providers who recognize the value a woman places on her time and capitalize on it are going to be successful in the years ahead. Creative healthcare facilities will establish patient loyalty by introducing programs and services which established conservative healthcare institutions seem to ignore.

3. *Women desire information.* Traditionally, women have been entrusted with the healthcare needed by them and their families. This responsibility requires maintaining a level of

knowledge about health affairs that other members of the family do not assume.

The "age of consumerism" has further supported this traditional woman's role. For women, like the rest of the consuming public, want information on which to base educated purchases. Healthcare is no exception.

The mass media had aided women enormously in their search for information about health. Sensing a hot topic, editors of magazines, newspapers, news and feature broadcast programs are more than happy to fill the information gap. The majority of Americans obtain their news from television; they obtain a great deal of medical and health information from it as well. Furthermore, the fastest growing magazines in ad revenues and circulation are health and fitness oriented: *Self, Prevention* and *American Health* were among the top ten magazines in 1985. As a result, the physician is no longer the sole source of medical information.

Similarly, other health-related groups have shown an interest in providing the consumer with information about health. Ancillary industries such as health food companies, the vitamin industry and the holistic health movement are just a few who offer alternative information resources. Their books, pamphlets, counseling, seminars and massive advertising campaigns feed a consumer movement demanding to know what the choices are.

Health information or misinformation, therefore, is readily available and plentiful. The task of becoming a credible source of health data then falls to the healthcare marketer, who must present the information in as intelligible and understandable a fashion as the mass media does.

The North Fulton Medical Center ads (exhibits 3-3 and 3-4), for instance, contribute to the woman's desire for information (and the marketer's image as a provider of reliable information).

Working while you're pregnant

Many women today keep working up until a very short time before they have their babies. All it takes is a little planning, and following the suggestions you'll find below.

It used to be that when a woman became pregnant she quit her job But no more.

That doesn't, however, mean a woman won't go through all the bodily and emotional changes that take place during pregnancy.

But it needn't be a problem. All it takes is a few simple steps such as the ones we've listed here

How to cope with morning sickness

It s more than difficult to work up to your full potential when you're nauseous.

But there are some ways of con trolling your out-of sorts stomach Most doctors, for example, rec ommend you keep some sort of non acid, non greasy food handy You might try keeping a box of crackers in your desk

Choose the childbirth course that suits you

North Fulton Medical Center offers a number of excellent courses that can make having a baby a more enjoyable experi ence. And don't worry We can make it convenient for you to attend, even with your work schedules. Want the details? Call 442 2220

- So you're thinking of having a baby
- Fertility awareness workshop
- Congratulations—you're pregnant
- Seven months and counting
- Big brother/big sister to be
- Positive infant parenting
- Health treats for tiny tots
- CPR and First Aid Techniques for infants and children

Some women get morning sick ness as soon as they arise. If this is the case, keep a box of crackers on your bedside table, so you can nibble before you even get up. And in cases where you're "morning sick" all day, you might try eating several small, bland meals instead of a larger one

In any case, it s important you do eat properly

Don't forget about good nutrition

It's easy to get so caught up in your work that you don't eat the way you should In any case, that's bad. When you're pregnant, it can be disastrous.

Force yourself to eat a well balanced diet of proteins and vege tables. Stay as far as possible from fatty foods.

Eat food high in fiber to calm hunger pangs and keep you regular.

Avoid beverages that are high in sodium or caffeine And eat plenty of cheese, yogurt cottage cheese and milk.

Control your cravings! As hard as it may be, it can be a source of too much of a good thing and a lot of extra calories.

Your doctor will probably also rec ommend a prenatal vitamin Take them religiously. You and your baby both need the extra help

Smoking

Don t do it. Smoking isn't good for anybody, but it can be especially bad for your baby.

We know it won t be easy to quit. You're under the pressure of work and surrounded by smoking co-workers.

But here are the facts. Smoking has been directly related to spon taneous miscarriages, stillbirths premature births and labor complications.

Smoking can also prevent you and your body from using certain vitamins and minerals in the foods you eat.

Women who smoke often have smaller babies, and there's an increased chance of brain damage You've probably always wanted to quit smoking Now you have the best reason ever to do it

Exercise

Years ago, pregnant women went to bed. But that's not you or you wouldn t be working

In any case, doctors say you need to get exercise. Don't sit at your desk too long; schedule several regular breaks during the day. Walk to lunch, or take a walk when you get home. (A good pair of support hose can help with that extra weight you're carrying around)

If you have a regular exercise program, you can continue it within reason. But, at the same time, we're not recommending you start jogging And if you feel

fatigued or uncomfortable at any time take it easy

Avoid stress

This may be the hardest part of working while you're pregnant

You have to learn to relax. We suggest you plan a time each day to sit back, forget about the problems of business, and spend a few minutes with your baby. You'll feel better, your baby will

be better off. And your work will still get done.

Never forget that even though you are working, you're pregnant The world will need to adjust a little for you

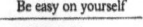
Be easy on yourself

Rest
You will need to rest more. Your body is going through a great many changes and you have a life growing inside you
That takes a lot of energy

Don't work too late
Keep an eye on the time. There s nothing you can t finish tomorrow.
(If there is, you need to change your schedule till the baby's born)

Stay away from stressful situations
This is one time in life when you need to control the stress of the work place Set aside time to take it easy on yourself each day

Don't strain yourself
You ll have enough difficulty getting around with your unaccustomed new figure Don't try to bend too far or lift heavy objects. Surely, someone will be more than willing to help you out

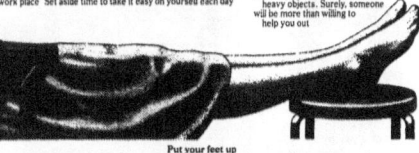

Put your feet up
This can be the best medicine in the world It gives you a chance to relax, get off your aching feet and spend a little time with your thoughts and what's going on inside you

For more information call 475-5552

Whatever information you need to know about working while you're pregnant, we can help (chances are, there is someone in the same condition here at the hospital).

That includes helping you find an obstetrician or a pediatrician or any other kind of doctor.

Just call our Physician Referral Service at 442 2208 Monday through Friday 8:30 a m to 5:00 p.m.

We'll give you a list of qualified doctors in the area from which you can choose

Having a baby is a 16-page brochure filled with information about one of life's most important events. If you d like a copy, give us a call or come by.

North Fulton Medical Center serves parts of Fulton, Cobb, DeKalb, Cherokee Forsyth, and Gwinnett counties We're on Highway 9, between Roswell and Alpharetta.

North Fulton Medical Center
Your hospital

11585 Alpharetta Street Roswell, Georgia 30076
A health care center of AMI

Exhibit 3-3

Having a baby

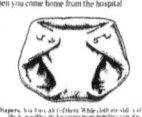

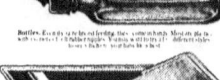

North Fulton Medical Center
Your hospital

11585 Alpharetta Street, Roswell, Georgia 30076
A health care center of AMI

Exhibit 3-4

4. *Women want to be in control.* The negative track record of such health issues as thalidomide, radical mastectomy, birth control pills, unnecessary hysterectomies, toxic shock syndrome, DES, cervical cancer, estrogen and more, has stimulated a growing distrust of the established healthcare community and, to a degree, of the medical profession.

In light of the growing loss of confidence in traditional healthcare, the marketplace is receptive to many kinds of alternatives, especially if they involve a greater degree of participation by the woman patient. Involvement for a woman means fully knowing the available options and then being able to select the best, in her mind, from among them. It may very well be that she will choose her family physician after all, but it's as likely that she will experiment with alternatives.

The implication for traditional healthcare is clear: women must feel they have choices, even within the limits of traditional medical practice. Not only for the birth of her child, where she can opt for standard delivery versus midwifery, the one-night stay versus the full three-day plan, but in choosing outpatient services, urgent care centers and comprehensive fitness/wellness programs for all members of the family as well. Women are making the important decisions based on the comforting knowledge that there are options and alternatives.

Notice, for example, how the copy in the North Memorial Medical Center and Rose Women's Center ads (exhibits 3-5 and 3-6) emphasizes choice and options.

5. *Women tend to be skeptical consumers.* As women become more educated, and therefore more confident in their ability to make informed decisions, they are resistant to manipulative efforts which exploit their vulnerabilities.

As value-oriented consumers of goods and services, they must be convinced from trustworthy sources that the provider has credible references. For this market, confidence and trust is won by consistently delivering a quality product.

Exhibit 3-5

The recent rush to promote women's health centers is a prime example of these two points. Many of these are really nothing more than breast diagnostic centers. While women are given the impression that the center will provide comprehensive health services, in reality the services are extremely limited. When the expectation far exceeds the satisfaction, a product or service has a limited life cycle.

In this case, as with some other healthcare products and services, the program is rushed to market before it has

OVER 100,000 WOMEN ARE CARRYING A CONCEALED WEAPON.

Breast cancer is the leading cancer killer of women in this country With this fact in mind, Rose Women's Center urges all women to have a mammogram. A mammogram is a safe, painless procedure to evaluate your breast tissue with x-rays. It can detect lumps so small that it would take years to discover them by physical examination. And since very early tumors are 95 percent curable, the importance of early detection can literally save your life

If you'd like to arrange for an appointment to have a mammogram at Rose Women's Center, call 320-2290 If you haven't already received your personal physician's approval, we'll be more than happy to arrange it for you If you don't have a personal physician, we'll put you in touch with one in your area.

Make an appointment now You've got nothing to lose, except a lot of anxiety

ROSE WOMEN'S CENTER
OUR STANDARDS ARE SIMPLY HIGHER.

ROSE MEDICAL CENTER
4567 EAST NINTH AVENUE, DENVER, COLORADO 80220
303-320-2290

Exhibit 3-6

been fully developed. This is always a disastrous mistake, one that should be avoided, for the costs are indeed high. Creating a demand for which there is no supply, or creating an expectation for which there is insufficient fulfillment, only alienates women. They are then hardly likely to believe in or choose your health care organization's other products or services.

6. *Women are value-oriented.* Women are cost-conscious, certainly, because they have to purchase many things with limited resources. For that very reason, women want to make sure they are getting value for their precious dollars. However, if a woman is convinced that a healthcare service is essential, that the facility is easily accessible and that it provides quality care, she is willing to spend a little more to obtain it. The promotion of the services, however, must be sincere, honest and compelling. Exaggerated claims, inflated emotions and inappropriate hype will be met with suspicion and disdain.

This "age of consumerism" is not a passing fad, but a reality which is certain to intensify over time. Betray a woman's confidence, build her expectations and not deliver on promises, and she will make her purchases (and her word-of-mouth recommendations) elsewhere.

7. *Women respond to the software of an issue rather than its hardware.* Information about the millions of dollars spent to build a new wing, the size of a specific department or the number of beds address the hardware of the healthcare facility. Women respond more enthusiastically to information that centers on direct *benefits* to them—"bigger" only in that there's no waiting, "newer" equipment so she can get her test results in minutes, "state of the art" technology so she can be assured of the safest, most accurate diagnosis.

When a health club advertisement focuses on the intrinsic benefits of membership, the message is clearly oriented to women. The club wants women to know that by joining, they are going to feel and look more beautiful, be able to work harder, live longer, lose weight or inches and feel better about themselves. They do not care what the health club owner has invested in equipment, only that the machine can help them have thinner thighs. In short, they do not care what *means* are available to achieve the benefit; their primary interest is in the *benefit* itself.

In tailoring your advertising message to women for any product or service, remember to skip illustrations of the emergency room or ambulance and avoid copy detailing the number of square feet of expanded space or the goals of a new fund-raising drive. These are not subjects that interest women, but are merely a means to an end.

8. *If women have children, those children are priorities.* The maternal instinct still runs strong and true.

In her research, Judith Langer, of Judith Langer and Associates, reports that women have traditionally harbored considerable guilt about buying for themselves, especially if they are married—and even more so if they are mothers. Not so when it comes to their children. Working mothers are particularly eager for their children to have every advantage they can buy. Health foods, a wide variety of lessons and quality brand clothing are favorite purchases for these mothers. For working mothers, brand name purchases are quicker and easier because they are shortcuts to assurance of quality merchandise.

Healthcare providers should take a clue from this research in marketing their own products and services. Establishing a pedigree of value helps enormously in cutting through resistance from this segment of the women's market. Generally, working women have little time and even less energy to shop comparatively, but will go directly to the provider who gives them the quality they are seeking.

The Humana Medfirst ad (exhibit 3-7) answers all those needs—with a humorous recognition of the mother's own need.

Children, especially the wished-for child, often function as a point of entry for the provider to capture the female audience, as the ad for The Laser Institute (exhibit 3-8) demonstrates.

Exhibit 3-7

The emphasis on marketing obstetrical services today is to capture the mother-to-be, for in so doing you also capture her husband, her current and future children, and in some cases her extended family, neighbors and friends. After a positive experience in one program, she will remain loyal and make sure others of her family enjoy the same service.

Exhibit 3-8

The copy for the Torrance Memorial Hospital ad (exhibit 3-9) seeks to capture child-bearing aged women from pre-pregnancy to parenthood.

A family is a challenging experience for women. Today's mother, especially if she is a part of the large population segment known as the "baby boom" generation, realizes how difficult it is to get ahead. For that reason, she wants her children to have a leg up on the competition, even before birth. Therefore, tremendous emphasis is put on giving the infant, toddler, child and teen every possible advantage now, to assist them in achieving as adults in tomorrow's world. If healthcare marketers can tap into this desire for quality service and beneficial information today, they will capture a substantial share of the market that will continue into the years ahead.

Mothers of intransigent teenagers or problem children respond to help which recognizes their predicament. Note the tagline with "best" in it, in the Psychiatric Institute of Washington ads (exhibits 3-10 and 3-11).

Having a baby and guiding its growth is a joyful experience But it also requires lots of preparation.

Fortunately, you can learn all you need to know from your doctor and Torrance Memorial Hospital Medical Center.

Torrance Memorial offers a complete schedule of classes on childbirth and child care. Our courses also deal with the physical and emotional health of new mothers And the adjustments required from other family members

Certified instructors will teach you about natural or cesarean childbirth. Lifesaving for infants and other safety strategies. Newborn care and toddler to preschool development.

Our Learn to Live™ programs also include managing the stresses of motherhood and a career. Fitness during and after pregnancy. Healthy ways for brothers and sisters to adapt to the new arrival.

So call 325-9110, Ext. 7560 for a current schedule of classes. Or write: Learn To Live, 3330 Lomita Blvd., Torrance, CA 90509-2935

Being prepared means taking better care of yourself and your child. Whether you're a new mother or expecting, we'll show you what to expect.

 Torrance Memorial Hospital Medical Center
Affiliated with Health Access Systems

Exhibit 3-9

If You Think Living With Your Difficult Child Is Tough, Try Living Without Her.

Last year more than 1 million teenagers ran away from home. Many still haven't been found. Some chose a more permanent way to escape. Over half a million tried to kill themselves.

For some teenagers summer makes it easier to cope. But for many, problems get worse. If your child's been spending a lot of time alone and withdrawn, summer days are longer, Emptier. Lonelier. She'll have more time to shut herself away. More time to dwell on her problems. If she's mad at the world and looking for a way to escape, she might decide that summer's a good time to run away. Or get into drugs and alcohol.

Depression and the drug addiction that often comes with it are illnesses. Diseases that can strike any child. As a parent it's important that you know that. And believe it. Many times the brightest kids — the ones who seem to have everything going for them — are victims. If you know your teenager has a problem — if you even suspect — don't blame yourself or hope the problem will disappear. Pick up the phone and call for help. It'll probably be one of the hardest things you'll ever have to do. But consider what might happen if you don't.

When you call us at The Psychiatric Institute of Washington, we'll talk about the problem with you and answer your questions. If you need more than information together we might decide you should bring your child in so we can talk with her, too. After an evaluation, if it turns out that she needs treatment, PIW has a reputation for being one of the best hospitals in the country. We have special programs for teenagers. With our team's guidance your child can learn how to deal with her problems. And get well again.

Teenage depression is a very serious problem. If you're just waiting for things to get better, you may be taking an awful risk. Sometimes problems go away by themselves. But other times children go away by themselves. Call The Psychiatric Institute of Washington at (202) 467-HOPE. *Psychiatric Institutes of America a subsidiary of National Medical Enterprises Inc*

THE PSYCHIATRIC INSTITUTE OF WASHINGTON
4460 MacArthur Boulevard, N.W., Washington, D.C., (202) 467-HOPE

Exhibit 3-10

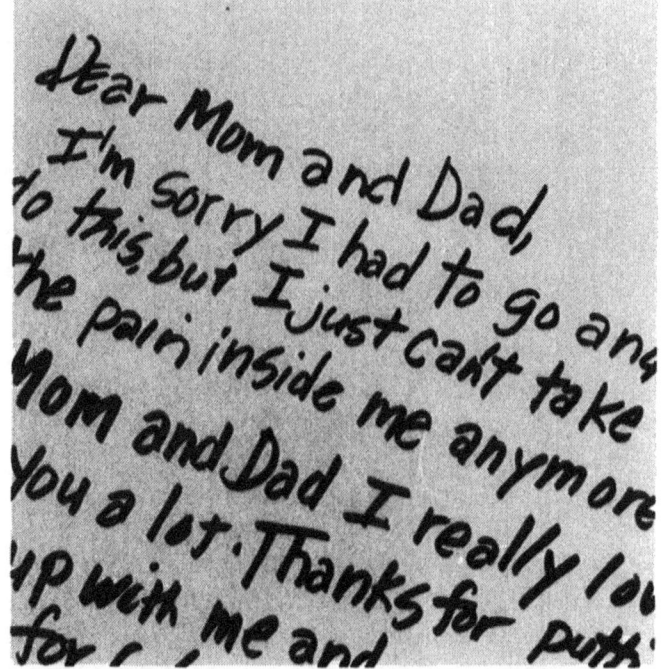

If Your Child Is Suffering From Sadness, Don't Wait Until You See The Handwriting On The Wall.

Exhibit 3-11

A natural service for the working morther is pediatrics and pediatric emergency care.

The ad from Bronson Methodist Hospital (exhibit 3-12) highlights precisely the emphasis marketers should make in appealing to the parent and her child. The headline is riveting. "My mom was really scared" hooks into every mom's deepest fears. It creates an image of the worst case scenario and invites the reader into every word. The opening copy, spoken from the first person, tells every mother exactly how frightened she was, how she resolved the problem and how Bronson was able to allay her fears with the most experienced childhood trauma and emergency medicine physicians in the area. Emphasizing the point that the hospital really knows about kids, the copy reassures mothers everywhere.

One of the most interesting findings in a focus group interview underscores the point. In talking with three distinct groups of women (ages 18-25, 25-40 and over 40) about a proposed women's facility, all the participants revealed that they would look for better quality goods and services for their *children* before they searched for it for themselves!

Women in the same focus group perceived that they could get more information from female medical practitioners. While many of the women acknowledged that having a female physician was desirable, it would *not* sufficiently motivate them to change from their traditional male healthcare provider.

However, when asked if they would choose female doctors for their *daughters*, most of the women appeared interested. Their rationale: they preferred their daughters to have a different experience than they had.

The ad for Doctor's Hospital in Tulsa, Oklahoma, presents information in an informative, easy-to-understand format (exhibit 3-13). This is the perfect ad to satisfy the kind of mother who wants to know, who needs information, who wants to be involved, when possible, in the healing process. This superbly developed ad understands a mother's concerns and

MY MOM WAS REALLY SCARED.

Mom "Scared? Panic stricken is more like it Bobby fell from his skates and hit his head And then he didn't move! I ran to him and then to the phone to call an ambulance— and all I could think was Bronson! They know about kids!"

Because Bronson does "know about kids" Bobby's fine now—back home—roller skating again Bronson Methodist Hospital has doctors and nurses skilled in childhood trauma and emergency medicine and the region's only Pediatric Intensive Care Unit.

Half of the deaths of children under 16 are caused by accidents With proper treatment during medical emergencies their odds for survival increase significantly. *Proper* treatment means they can't be treated simply as "little adults." Proper treatment means special kinds and sizes of equipment It means special training, such as our Pediatric Intensive Care Nurses receive—more than 200 hours of it And it means the skills of physicians trained in specialized pediatric care All of these pediatric specialists are available round the clock every day of the year.

Yes, we really "know about kids" and if you'd like to know more about our special pediatric services call 616 383 6328

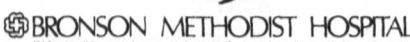

BRONSON METHODIST HOSPITAL

252 East Lovell Street • Kalamazoo Michigan 49007 A member of Bronson Healthcare Group Inc

Exhibit 3-12

Bugs that sting, plants that poison, and what to do when they do

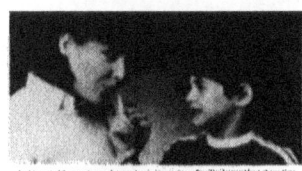

In this part of the country, you're sure to run across an unfamiliar bug or plant at one time or another. The more you know about them, the better off you are.

Warm, sunny weather inspires us all but the staunchest homebodies to get outside and play, do yardwork, or go exploring. But be careful. If you get too close to Mother Nature she could sap you with some real toxic trouble.

You can have your fun in the sun safely though, with a bit of information. And Doctors' Hospital wants to help. Because the more you know, the more calmly you can react and the better off the victim will be.

The 6 most common stings

Everyone knows what a nuisance bees, wasps and hornets can be, especially around gardens, garbage cans and swimming pools. To avoid them, don't wear bright clothes or sweet smelling toiletries. And always wear long pants and shoes while mowing the lawn or working outside.

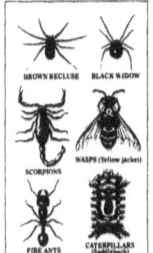

Any ant can give you an uncomfortable bite, and ruin your picnic, but the most troublesome is the quick-tempered fire ant. He latches on with powerful jaws, then stings repeatedly. This attack leaves his victim with red rings that turn into blisters, often taking 10 days to heal. One bite is bad enough, so be careful of disturbing an entire mound of these savage little ants.

Scorpions may look deadly, but the ones found in this part of the country are relatively harmless. However, they're larger than most stinging creatures and can produce a lot of pain. Watch out for them at night, when they search for food.

Stinging caterpillars have fine hairs that break off and inject venom when brushed against the skin. The most common of these is the saddleback caterpillar, which is easy to recognize by the "saddle" mark on its mid-section: bright green and brown colors and "horns" on both ends.

Can stings be really dangerous?

Yes, they can be lethal if you have a hypersensitive reaction to the venom. (Death could also occur in a non-sensitive person, especially a child, if he were stung enough times.)

Each year, more than 2 million Americans are treated for allergic reactions to insect stings, and between 50 and 100 deaths are reported.

Symptoms of a severe reaction include a general swelling of the body, hives, shortness of breath and nausea. Death results from the body's inability to supply blood to the brain, or by asphyxiation because of hives in the throat.

What to do if you're stung

If a stinger is left in the wound, gently remove it by scraping. *Do not squeeze the stinger,* as this will force out more venom. Remove caterpillar spines with a piece of tape. Clean the area with an antiseptic like rubbing alcohol. For the redness, swelling and itching of a mild reaction to most any insect sting, apply an ice pack and a paste of baking soda and water. Take aspirin and antihistamine for discomfort.

When an allergic reaction occurs, seek medical attention immediately. If you know you're allergic to certain insect stings, wear a medic-alert tag and keep an emergency treatment kit nearby.

Dealing with bugs that bite

Biting insects can cause problems because of the poisons they inject or because of the diseases they spread.

The most common dangerous spiders in the Southwest are the black widow and brown recluse. The black widow is recognizable by the red hourglass shape on its abdomen. The brown recluse is marked by a fiddle-shaped design.

Black widows bite only when their web is disturbed or when they're provoked. There's no initial pain or swelling, so you may not even realize you've been bitten. But in as little as 15 minutes a numbing pain develops around the bite, accompanied by muscle spasms and abdominal cramps.

Because she injects so little venom, the black widow is not considered deadly for most healthy adults, but extra precaution must be taken with the very young and the very old.

The brown recluse likes to hide in cloth-ing and delivers an immediately painful bite which can cause death if untreated. His venom is not quite so lethal as that of the black widow, but it has an effect that hers doesn't: it produces hard-to-heal lesions that can lead to extensive tissue damage.

If symptoms of a black widow or brown recluse spider bite occur, seek medical attention immediately. Go to the Doctors' Hospital Emergency Room.

Plants can cause problems, too

It's surprising just how many plants are poisonous. They can cause irritations, illness, and in some cases, death. Even parts of the plants we eat every day can be harmful. For example, the leaves and stems of tomato plants and the green parts and sprouts of potatoes are poisonous. And if you eat too many apple seeds, you could be poisoned by cyanide.

The best way to prevent plant poisonings is to know the plants in your yard and home, and never eat any wild plants. Store bulbs and seeds away from children, and teach them to keep plants out of their mouths.

What should you do if you think someone has been poisoned by a plant? First call the local poison center for advice. Then get the victim to Doctors' Hospital Emergency Room as soon as possible.

Bring along samples of the plant or plants you think caused the poisoning. They will help the doctor identify the plant and choose the correct treatment.

7 dangerous plants to watch out for

Here are a few of this area's most common poisonous plants. Seek medical attention if you suspect poisoning by any of them (including poison ivy if the reaction is severe).

CAROLINA YELLOW JASMINE. Most intoxications occur in children from sucking on the flowers of this woodland vine. Its poison produces muscle weakness and contraction, dizziness, drooping eyelids and dryness of the mouth.

DUMBCANE. This potted houseplant (along with the Philodendron) is responsible for more cases of symptomatic distress in children than all other plants. Full of needle-sharp chemical crystals, it causes immediate pain, swelling and blisters in the mouth if chewed. A spoonful of sugar may help but it's best to get medical attention since swelling could block breathing passages.

RHODODENDRON. These pink, red or white flowering bushes include the azalea, popular around houses and parks. The poison is in the leaves and flowers; attacks the nervous system and causes vomiting, diarrhea and weakness. In severe cases, the heart rate slows, blood pressure drops and death results.

NIGHTSHADE. All parts of this weed are poisonous, and it has been known to live up to its name. Children are most likely to eat the berries and will develop a scratchiness of the throat, nausea, diarrhea and pain.

POISON HEMLOCK. Lacy leaves and umbrella-shaped white flower clusters make this lethal roadside weed easy to identify. The seeds and leaves are the most poisonous parts, but children have become ill from using the hollow stems as blowpipes. Its poisons cause trembling, loss of muscle control, a slowing of the heartbeat, and unconsciousness. Death occurs when the breathing muscles fail.

POISON IVY. "Leaflets three, let it be." A wise saying since this plant (and its relative, poison oak) causes an allergic reaction in 7 out of 10 people. In 24 to 48 hours, victims develop a blistery rash and almost unbearable itching. Wash promptly, apply wet cold compresses and use Calamine lotion for relief.

FOXGLOVE. Easily recognized by its tubular purple or pink flowers, all parts of this ornamental plant contain poisons. One of its irritants causes burning of the mouth and intestinal distress; another is responsible for major toxic effects on the heart.

For information call 744-4000 or your doctor

It's better to be safe than sorry, so if there's ever a doubt about an insect or plant poisoning, get medical attention immediately.

If you have specific questions about potentially harmful insects or plants, call your doctor.

Whatever the subject, if it has to do with health, your family doctor is the best person to talk to.

If you don't have a family doctor we can help. Call our physician referral service at 744-4000 and we'll give you a list from which to choose.

For your free copy of our Emergency Medical Directory, call 744-4000

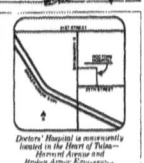

Doctors' Hospital is conveniently located in the Heart of Tulsa— Harvard Avenue and Broken Arrow Expressway.

Doctors' Hospital
Your hospital

2323 South Harvard Avenue Tulsa, Oklahoma 74114
A health care center of **AMI**

Exhibit 3-13

communicates with her in a sophisticated, intelligent and respectful way. Furthermore, this kind of ad positions the hospitals as an ally in the health process, an authority on health issues, and a resource should there ever be a health problem. It satisfies in every regard the Yuppie Mom as well as every other category of woman.

CAN MEN MARKET TO WOMEN?

One of the most stubbornly held beliefs in advertising is that men are better suited to marketing high tech, automotive and sports accounts, and that women are better qualified to create advertising for cosmetics, fashion and food.

Not necessarily.

Time and again, women have brought fresh and innovative perspectives to the stereotypical male domains, often picking up on marketing opportunities missed by their male counterparts. A cursory review of the personnel of leading consumer advertising companies will reveal how substantially women are represented and contribute their talents and ideas to the achievement of client goals.

The question is, is the reverse also true?

In general consumer marketing to women, account executives consisting of male team members also create memorable, effective advertising.

However, in marketing healthcare services to women, some men feel inadequate to tackle the sensitive, personal, underlying issues implicit in advertising OB/GYN, breast diagnostic screening or long-term care for elderly parents.

Certainly there are many men who have very little experience—and even less knowledge—about these "female" health concerns and what motivates the female consumer to purchase these types of services. Men often have considerable trepidation about addressing the opposite sex in these matters.

Part of their reluctance has to do with their training from childhood. Part of it has to do with the success of consciousness-raising over the last ten years. As a result, it is not unusual to find men stumbling over themselves to make sure they don't say or do anything that will offend women. They may, for example, apologize for perfectly innocent remarks they inadvertently made but which they feel women might resent. This self-conscious approach to communicating with women can sometimes be a hurdle to creating advertising expressly for them. And sometimes not.

In one instance, a male copywriter was presented with the marketing reports, creative strategy, analysis and media recommendations for a variety of programs targeted to women and to be marketed by a healthcare facility. Special pains were taken to explain the particular sensitivities, taboo subjects and sacred cows that, depending on the item, needed to be included or excluded from the copy. The final result—a delighted client who was positive the copy was written by a woman!

By the same token, a female copywriter was unable to complete a similar project because she could not view it objectively. Rather, her own prejudices, prior experiences and predispositions clouded the copy. The assignment became an exercise in self-analysis for her instead of the production of good advertising.

Essentially, then, the gender of the marketing person or creative team member makes little difference. What does matter—and what makes all the difference—is whether the advertising team can be objective, sensitive and tuned in to the consumer of a product or service. Be it a sophisticated healthcare computer software product or an intimate personal healthcare service, it is vital to look beyond the features of a product to assess its special benefits to its target audience. Identification of the particular benefits that are most important to the target audience(s) is paramount in order to create compelling advertising. A person's sex, background and previous experience may be of value; but it is his or her *clear, critical thinking* that is the basis of effective advertising and advertising effectively to women.

And because each client, each market, each product or service is different, and segments of the women's population are so varied, it is possible to create fresh approaches within the same category continually—and without ever exhausting the limitless numbers of messages that would appeal to your market.

What it takes to achieve this is a clear, critical mind. Good advertising is genderless; the message to women is implicit—regardless of who creates it.

WHO CREATED WHAT? A CHALLENGE FOR SEXIST THINKERS

The two blocks of copy that follow were prepared by two different creative teams. Who created each, men or women? The answer is on page 145.

What you *don't* know can hurt you.

Last year, thousands of women lost their lives to breast cancer. Yet hundreds of thousands more successfully detected the problem early enough to take appropriate steps to conquer it.

Through routine breast self-examination and a scheduled

mammogram, every woman can enjoy the peace of mind that comes from knowledge of her body. And we have taken some important steps to help in this learning process.

South Bay Hospital is pleased to introduce the safest and most modern mammographic unit available—the XERG II. Superior to other systems in technology and design, the XERG II system was specifically chosen by South Bay Hospital because it emits the lowest amount of radiation per exposure with excellent image detail. Our new mammograph unit also includes a separate waiting room, private examination room, and female technologists to assist you.

Now the fight against breast cancer is safer, more effective, and more comfortable. So don't hide from yourself. A little bit of knowledge goes a long way toward the early detection of a disease that knows no limits.

Don't believe everything you fear.

Perhaps no other concern affects a woman with quite the same intensity as breast health. Or has as many implications for her femininity, close relationships and family response. For those very reasons, the issue can become one many choose to block, to deny, to view only in the extreme. At————— Hospital, we know how compelling those feelings can be. And how important it is to confront them before they become self-fulfilling prophecies.

Today, advances in early detection can find tissue masses years before they become lumps detectable by self-examination. New techniques in low dosage mammography are more accurate and extremely safe. And new techniques in treatment require less radical solutions than in the past.

But there is no other factor more important than early detection. Not one.

Unfortunately, many women let their fears postpone routine checkups until the problem becomes much more serious. Although, in point of fact, almost 90% of all women *never* develop breast cancer.

If you're 30 years of age or older, regular checkups with your physician as well as clear information on breast health are two things you shouldn't put off any longer.

At————————Hospital, the charge for low dose mammography, and professional radiologist's reading is a small price to pay for assurance.

You've heard and read a great deal on the subject. Now it's time for an accurate, personal determination for yourself.

Do it today. And stop believing everything you fear.

Market Research Is More Than Asking the Right Questions

Nowhere in the advertising process is money more wisely spent and more foolishly not spent than in the area of market research.

For some reason, healthcare advertisers have a reluctance to invest the dollars and sense to find out who their market is, if the market wants or needs the "product" they are offering and how the product or service is perceived by the consumer. When advertisers rely on hunches and gut feelings for the themes and concepts of their messages, the essential first step of proper market research is bypassed. And sometimes when research *is* done, interpretation may be faulty and can lead to very expensive marketing mistakes. Witness the colossal failure of the Edsel as a never-to-be-forgotten bad example. And, finally, even with an arsenal of sophisticated market research, the right weapon in the wrong hands can miss the mark.

If market research is basic to advertising and marketing healthcare products and services, then market research on healthcare's chief purchasers assumes even greater importance. *Women are the target audience for the majority of programs, products and services that healthcare advertisers have to offer.*

Yet, in researching the women's market, proceed with caution. As we approach the end of this century, researchers are discovering that women are not a homogeneous mass audience. The incredible number of roles women play during each phase of their lives make women complex and moving targets. They cannot simply be categorized by age, socio-economic level, educational background or race. They are strongly influenced by the prevailing attitudes of their families, peers, community and their own growing independence resulting from their increasing roles as breadwinners. And the changes women everywhere are experiencing will accelerate in the years ahead as their "revolution" permeates all levels of society.

THE VALUE OF RESEARCH IN MARKETING TO WOMEN

Solid research (and even better interpretation of the data) produces the foundation on which to build a well-targeted marketing program aimed at segments of the women's market. Why?

- *Market research avoids the danger of tunnel vision.* Regardless of our sex, we all harbor certain assumptions about women. Most likely, they are based on stereotypes and perceptions of women with whom we are—or have been—associated. We may think we know what makes women tick, but we must avoid that trap, especially as we narrow our focus to segmented marketing. Market research will help identify the differences between perception and reality.

- *Market research can confirm hunches.*
Even if the market survey substantiates exactly what you thought, it is far better to have quantifiable data to support your assumptions than to bet your ad budget on your "gut feelings."

    And don't become complacent and bypass a repetition of the research process the next time you bring a product or service to the marketplace. Unless all the variables are the same—and that's most unlikely!—the subtleties you overlook may mean the difference between success or failure of your campaigns.

- *Market research minimizes risk-taking.*
Good, effective advertising, to be seen and heard above the clutter of general advertising and competitive healthcare advertising specifically, involves some risks. Since advertising is costly, market research should be considered the insurance you need to turn this expense into an investment.

    First, it serves as a means of tracking reasons why an advertising campaign or marketing program is successful—or a failure. If the campaign is wildly successful, market research can be deemed as a valid contribution to the effort. If the campaign fails to achieve its expected results, then market research provides a record from which to reformulate the sponsoring healthcare facility's marketing position in the field, the validity of the creative concept employed and the use of media. It is possible, of course, that the market research itself was off target or misinterpreted and needs to be restructured.

    Next, valid market research provides reassurance when the advertising costs are reviewed. If the market research indicated there is a viable market for your product or service, then spending for print, broadcast and collateral materials to reach that market makes sense. As any good poker player will tell you, you've covered your bet and increased the odds of winning in a rather high stakes game.

Finally, valid market research enables the health-care facility to avoid costly errors in product and program design and reduces mistakes when bringing a finished product to the marketplace. Rather than second-guessing, market research can point the way to any necessary adjustments in the components of a program or a service before it is introduced. A research nugget may be as simple as learning that women prefer evening hours at the facility that extend to 9 p.m. rather than 8 p.m., or as sophisticated as tracking the precise referral patterns used by women in seeking medical services in the community.

- *Market research identifies market niches to win that competitive edge.*
  Market research may also uncover previously unknown information as well as reaffirming the value of the proposed program or service. As healthcare marketing matures, greater emphasis will be placed on segmenting audiences within the target market. Women over 30 are an important audience for a proposed service, but women in that age category may have important differences that must be addressed, such as marital status or the number of children living at home. The marketing of these "niches" presents opportunities for taking a leading role in providing healthcare services to the women in them.

Caution. Market research, if used appropriately and interpreted wisely, is a useful tool, but it is only one tool; it is not a substitute for shrewd decision-making and astute entrepreneurial thinking. Don't let market research overshadow common sense. If survey results, for example, conflict with opposing solid evidence, perhaps the format or implementation of the research needs further examination. Avoid using market research as a crutch or an excuse for postponing a campaign.

PLANNING AND CONDUCTING MARKET RESEARCH

Before investing in market research, devote some time to thinking through exactly what information you will need and how it will be utilized. In this way, you will have a clearer idea of what you know, what you need to know and how to accomplish the task efficiently.

1. *Start with what you know.* You and your colleagues already know a great deal from your experiences in your marketplace. In addition, your healthcare organization has probably collected data on the population you serve. Try these sources first:

- Current demographic data is easily and inexpensively obtained through the chamber of commerce, your local newspaper or broadcast stations.

- Examine records of admissions, patient census, utilization patterns and payment sources that already exist within your organization.

- Talk to your staff: telephone operators, receptionists, nurses, aides, volunteers. Often, they are more than happy to discuss areas of patient and program satisfaction and other areas that need improvement. You may also wish to take informal written surveys among these groups.

- Talk to the data processing manager. A knowledgeable resource, this person can provide you with all types of

valuable information and guide you in establishing forms
and formats for processing future data.

- Search the literature. More than likely, a nearby health
science, medical school or university library has
indexed health literature. Healthcare and hospital
marketing publications may have already covered your
area of concern in published articles and studies. Local
and national magazines and newspapers are also certain to contain stories on health topics, and while not as
comprehensive, will be helpful in providing a consumer's viewpoint.

2. *Separate Assumptions from Facts.* From the data you col-
lect, you and your colleagues will accumulate many pre-
conceived ideas. List all these separately and title them
"assumptions." Later, compare them to the facts to discover
how great the differences are between them.

- Determine what facts you need that you don't already
know.

- Write down all questions that have not been answered.
The list may be small or quite extensive. Then ask, "Is
there a question or questions I don't know enough to
ask?" If the response is "yes," decide if you need more
qualitative or quantitative information.

In other words, do you need more numbers or subjective views?
Usually you will need qualitative information first. From that,
you will build the format for obtaining quantitative data.
Women are generally very straightforward with their opinions,
ideas and suggestions, and therefore make excellent subjects
for the kind of initial qualitative research you desire to begin a
market study project.

KNOW THE TYPES OF RESEARCH AVAILABLE
AND CONDUCT IT CAUTIOUSLY

Many excellent books and articles have been published on the kinds and validity of various market studies. Before engaging a professional market research company, do some background reading and familiarize yourself and your staff with the types of studies that are available. However, remember: you are preparing for a specific study for a specific purpose. For the women's market, an important resource is the focus group.

Focus Groups

Focus groups are especially valuable for obtaining the soft information—feelings, impressions, suggestions, opinions— that often are the real reasons why a product or service is purchased or used.

A focus group is a professionally-conducted brainstorming session. Carefully selected representatives *from your target audience* are invited to meet to evaluate and discuss a selected topic. It is important for the leader or facilitator of the group to make the participants feel comfortable enough to express themselves with honesty and candor. Therefore, focus groups are usually held in a neutral site and chaired by a neutral leader.

These are the advantages of a focus group:

- Women disclose their thinking/reasoning patterns in considering the topic under discussion.

- They reveal a sensitivity to nuances or shades of opinions.

- Many alternatives to the same problem are suggested.

- A particular topic can be deeply explored.

The disadvantages of a focus group are:

- Information is not ranked or listed by priority; each person's opinions and thoughts are equally valuable.

- Information cannot necessarily be projected to the population of women (and men) as a whole. It only applies to that group of women at that time.

- Skill and time are required. Focus groups can easily consume several days for their preparation and actual development. The leader must be adept at keeping the group's discussion on the subject and at probing for true feelings.

Successful focus groups are those that produce valuable, honest information and are the result of:

- Professional moderators and a discriminating selection of participants and planned sessions.

- Pre-set goals and objectives. The kind of information sought from the sessions must be determined before the meetings take place.

- Taped recordings and written transcripts must be made. Even a superlative note taker cannot capture the emotional charges that certain discussions arouse.

- Formal reports. In addition to the transcripts, an interpretive report summarizing the points and recommendations that emerged from the session should be printed.

Once the qualitative information is obtained, reorganize the data into a format to test, make projections and develop measurable goals and objectives against a larger sample group of women for verification. (An example of a focus group report appears in the Appendix.)

Surveys

Many types of survey designs have been developed and your choice should depend upon your purpose and reporting format needs. The most popular types are interviews which can be done by telephone, mail or in person. Again, the specific design of the questionnaire will depend on what type of information you are seeking, how it will be used and how it will be reported.

These are the advantages of an interview/questionnaire:

- Hard data on which to base projections is produced.
- Data from which other data can be extracted is available.
- Data is ranked and items are weighed for marketing strategy decisions.
- Demographic information to further define market segments is produced.

The disadvantages of questionnaires are:

- Need for valid sample. The size and scope of the survey design may not accurately reflect the market segment. Danger in overinterpreting or interpolating too much from the data.
- Respondent may choose one item over others without explaining her reasons for doing so.

Questionnaires can become a first step in a dialogue with potential patients. Although the following ad for Daniel Freeman Memorial Hospital (exhibit 5-1) was not published, it demonstrates a concern for women's preferences.

By now, it should be apparent that virtually all market research has its limitations. Short of personally contacting every woman in your target market, research can at best produce a statistically significant guide to the preferences of women as revealed by their responses to specific questions and issues. However, when designed well, implemented properly and used as a research guide, it can provide significant insights into unforeseen marketing opportunities.

Exhibit 5-1

INTERPRETING RESULTS—THE MOMENT OF TRUTH

Gathering and reporting the data is one function of market research, but interpreting the meaning of that research is quite another. It requires another kind of talent. This dimension is crucial to the success or failure of the entire marketing program. Beyond the numbers, knowledge of the buyers' emotions or "hot buttons"—forces which will ultimately motivate action—is what counts in marketing and advertising.

Research is significant in revealing issues which will determine how to market and to whom it should be directed. Because healthcare has many audiences today, marketing aimed directly at women may not be the first or best direction for the proposed product or service. In the beginning, especially, certain segments of the female population want the comfort of an official "seal of approval" of the program from physicians or respected healthcare institutions.

For other segments of the broad women's population, the "image" of quality, innovation, elitism, sophistication or feminism assumes major importance—surpassing all other concerns. For still others, value, convenience and word-of-mouth recommendations will be the ultimate appeal. Successful campaigns hinge on correctly reading the emotional issues that motivate the women and translating them into appealing messages. Determining these issues before a single illustration is drawn or a single word written begins with targeting the woman and accurately identifying her healthcare concerns.

HEALTHCARE IS NOT AN IMPULSE PURCHASE

To successfully advertise healthcare, one must understand two basic truths: (1) advertising cannot stimulate demand; it can only capture a share of the market for a product or service and, (2) advertising is most effective in introducing products or services to satisfy an unmet consumer need.

In marketing to women, another essential truth applies: *healthcare is something women tend to postpone buying.* Although statistics disclose that women tend to be the greatest users of healthcare, it does not seem to be a high priority in her own world. Typically, a woman will begrudge time spent seeing physicians. She even resents visiting them for her own illnesses. This procrastination, especially in the areas of preventive healthcare, shows up most noticeably among two segments of the female population: career/working women and mothers.

Career/working women juggle other priorities too much to find the time for healthcare considerations. If this woman is also a mother, the postponement is more intense—not for her children but for herself. The busier the woman, the more "permission" she needs to slow down and take care of her own health needs. Indeed, she may secretly wish—albeit with guilt—to be ill enough to warrant a sick day or two, which would afford a respite, a chance to relax, to catch up on some reading, to forget the household chores. In her view, she almost needs the excuse of serious illness as a reason for what she might consider a self-indulgence.

Mothers, whether working or not, participate in a similar kind of mindset, but do tend to make sure their children are well cared for. An illness or injury has to be something serious—or existing more than a day or two—to allow the mother to put her needs as a top priority.

THE DILEMMA OF NON-IMPULSE PRODUCT MARKETERS

Healthcare is not alone in offering a product or service whose ultimate purchaser is not impulsive in his or her action. At least two consumer categories face similar marketing problems: automobile tires and funeral homes.

The purchase of tires is infrequent, often put off, in fact, until the time is convenient or it becomes absolutely necessary. People generally do not buy tires unless they are really ready to, and many will take weeks to shop comparatively, seeking the best price. As a result, a tire purchase can be months in the making, despite the ads for tire sales which appear almost daily in local newspapers. One tire dealer attempted to solve the problem in this way: along with the weekly "specials," his ad included short editorials about when, where and how to buy tires. This advertising approach reached two audiences at once: those ready to buy that week and those still thinking about it. By steadily supplying basic information about tires, potential buyers will be predisposed to think of his company as a leading candidate in their universe of choices and to pay more attention to his specials when they cross over to the "ready-to-buy" market category.

The same marketing problem faces the funeral industry. Few persons want to make "pre-need" funeral arrangements for themselves or their loved ones, much as the funeral industry advocates doing so. But when the moment of need comes, the bereaved family wants all the information and all the support possible to help them with their decisions. Whom do you call? Who makes a referral? Who takes care of the arrangements? How much does it cost? What are the choices? The only marketing/advertising message that comes to the consumer's mind at the time is the recollection that the funeral home has a credible, reliable reputation within the community.

It is for this reason that one sees so many bus stop benches and billboards which simply advertise the availability and trustworthiness of a funeral home. Yet, it is the carefully constructed image of confidence, consciously developed over a long period of time, that finally results in the call for information and then the sale at a time when the decision to purchase the service is imperative.

. . . And the Implications

This is, in essence, the plight of the healthcare facility advertiser. How does it get a potential female patient to think about healthcare *before* her need for it arises, so that her decision does not have to be made in haste and to insure that she'll use its particular product and service?

In order to begin the process, healthcare marketers must:

1. Build a relationship. The provider must establish a

relationship with the potential women's market to build enduring trust and confidence. That means advertising consistently, so when her need arises, she'll become a patient.

2. Be Patient. Most healthcare facilities are eager to see immediate results for their advertising expenditures, and want them to show up on the bottom line much sooner than reality normally allows. Just because you advertise the convenience, accessibility and moderate cost of an Urgent Care Center or a specific department in your facility, remember that a potential buyer may not need those services until six months later when her child wakes up at midnight with a painful earache. Unless the Urgent Care Center is advertising "specials" on school/camp examinations or blood tests, it's unrealistic to expect throngs at the facility's threshold.

What's important to appreciate is that there are two types of advertising: image and response-generating. In marketing to women, one really needs to do both to reap the maximum benefit. But the advertising must be continuous and sustained because the decisions to use the services are often delayed. Women need to trust in their choice, even if made in haste. If that trust in your facility hasn't been cultivated, they may hesitate and choose to go elsewhere.

WORD-OF-MOUTH ADVERTISING: MOST POTENT

By far, the most effective advertising motivator among women is word-of-mouth recommendations, especially for healthcare. Every piece of research indicates, almost without exception, that a direct recommendation from a friend or relative is the single most important factor women use in deciding whether to try a particular product, service or doctor.

To illustrate and reinforce the point: in one focus group

devoted to evaluating the obstetrical services of various hospitals within a market area, one of the women participants had delivered her first baby at a hospital which competes with the one undertaking the study. She extolled the virtues of her experience with excitement and enthusiasm. She was absolutely rapturous and sincere in her appreciation of the treatment she received at that neighboring hospital. In fact, she communicated her praise in such a compelling way that in five minutes she had convinced other focus group members who were pregnant to have their babies there! The researchers spent the remainder of the session probing for the reasons for that woman's unequivocal endorsement.

So where does this leave advertising and marketing activities? For one thing, it means that EVERY contact between patient and healthcare staff—from the admitting clerk, billing office and custodian to the medical personnel—is not only a point of delivery of some specific service but a *marketing contact* as well. The patient who is treated with respect and consideration today will return tomorrow, and is most likely to recommend the same doctor, hospital or healthcare service to friends. As one woman explained, "If I have a health problem, I ask around and talk to friends to see if they've had a similar problem, and, if so, I ask who they saw to take care of it. If they had a good experience, then I am more inclined to make an appointment with that doctor (go to that hospital, use that service)."

Advertising of course plays an important role in enhancing or reinforcing the influential word-of-mouth recommendation as well as in introducing those new healthcare services not sufficiently known to be promoted by satisfied patients. Advertising does reach out to create recognition, communicate availability and invite trial use. It can bring the patient to the door. What happens to the patient once inside is crucial, for in treating one woman well, the doctor or the institution is really marketing quality to many, many others. "Closing the loop," or attending to a quality delivery cycle, is discussed in detail in Chapter 8.

GETTING THE WORD OUT: THE CHALLENGES

With the many different segments (and their differing needs) existing in the women's market, the way to reach each population requires, by necessity, many different media strategies. According to Rena Bartos (in her book, *The Moving Target*), "The days when the media planner listened politely to some abstract definition of marketing segments and then proceeded to force it all into the cookie-cutter pattern of 'any housewife, 18 to 49' are gone." She describes the media potential of the 1980s with two words: "challenge" and "opportunity."

The importance of personal relationships. As we've suggested, a woman's first line of information comes from personal relationships and recommendations, either through friends and family or through her physician. She will look to her doctor as an authority for all health-related matters and, if satisfied by his or her explanation and guidance, will look no further.

The emerging "need to know" attitude. As women become more receptive to all kinds of new information and knowledge, such as finance, travel, high-tech equipment, investments, and so on, it is only natural that they are viewing health as another field to know and understand better. This emerging attitude (full-blown for some women) is both a blessing and a curse for the healthcare provider. For a long time, doctors and hospitals held the franchise. They released medical information at their own discretion, being careful not to give too much information for fear it might confuse the patient. They sincerely believed the patient wouldn't understand—or didn't want to understand—much of it. Hospitals and physicians set the rules and the patient acquiesced with varying reactions.

Now doctors are confronted with the questioning minds of

their female patients. Women want to know about the efficacy of a certain medication or treatment, its side effects, what alternatives are available, what happens if she doesn't take it and more. Not satisfied with just the doctor's explanation, they read (or have already read) a variety of health-related articles in magazines and newspapers, watch television news reports and special documentaries on health topics, listen to radio talk shows featuring doctors and purchase countless health, fitness and disease-related fiction and nonfiction books. They know about all kinds of alternative medicine, services and experiments that have surfaced in recent years. It is no wonder that doctors and hospital staffs are obliged to devote time to explaining, defending or advocating a specific treatment to a skeptical patient, rather than just administering it.

INTERNAL MARKETING— CLOSING THE LOOP

Kristine Peterson
President, K. E. Peterson & Associates

In simplest terms, it doesn't matter what service you market to women if—once they've experienced it—their great expectations are dashed.

Today, alert healthcare marketers are paying equal attention to their external *and* internal marketing programs. Internal marketing is the effort to teach employees that the service organization's mission is to provide quality service. Internal marketing educates and motivates employees to insure the customers' needs will be met and their expectations will be exceeded.

A successful internal marketing program is characterized by:

- Strategies that make quality service and customer satisfaction the highest priorities;

- Values that demonstrate a strong commitment to employee as well as customer satisfaction;

- Programs that develop human resources, recognizing that employees are the most valuable marketing resource;

- Systems that allow service to be provided easily and quickly;

- Feedback systems that report if customers' needs and expectations are being met.

Finally, to be successful, your organization must be innovative and responsive. You must be ready to change the strategies you conceive and services you design. Without reliable market research and thorough service audits, you can lose touch with the driving factors of customer motivation. New customer needs must be continually anticipated as changes take place. What customers say about their experiences will indicate what services need to be enhanced or modified.

CUSTOMER EXPECTATIONS

An intense preoccupation with customer satisfaction is a key characteristic of successful service companies and applies especially to healthcare provider organizations because people have such high expectations of this industry. The reasons are many:

- The high costs of medical care have created a public mind-set; if getting well costs this much, the care better be good.

- The media portrayal of medical care and facilities; the

"Marcus Welby" syndrome is pervasive—consumers expect (if not demand) instant restoration to their full health.

- A long-standing perception that healthcare's sole mission is to be benevolent and personally attentive.

- People who are sick perceive their problems to be the only ones; regardless of other circumstances, they especially are entitled to personal care.

Women are especially responsive to providers who are sensitive to their needs as well as those of their families. Given the previous insensitivity of medical providers to women's health issues, such as pregnancy, pre-menstrual syndrome or the psychological trauma of breast and uterine cancer, it is easy to see why women have come to demand special considerations for their healthcare needs.

Because a medical yardstick has not been created for consumers to measure the performance of one provider versus another, increased importance has been placed on the tangible measurements of quality. While consumers' impressions are influenced by the appearance, food and other amenities of a facility, three primary needs shape the customer's expectation of what his healthcare experience should include. Basically, healthcare consumers want:

- To be treated courteously and respectfully;

- To have their needs responded to promptly;

- To receive sufficient information to restore their sense of control.

In the past, providers have encouraged ignorance because the "mystique" engendered a more dependent relationship and fostered greater passivity and compliance on the part of patients. Due to the massive amounts of information on health and wellness available through the media, consumers are now more knowledgeable and are more assertive in their quest for information. An informed consumer is less likely to sue the hospital or physician, since improved communication generates greater satisfaction and assuages his need for control.

YOUR GOAL—TO EXCEED EXPECTATIONS

Simply meeting expectations is not enough. Your goal must be to exceed them. An interesting paradox comes into play when we consider customer expectations.

When expectations are met, nobody notices.

In other words, if customers expect employees to be courteous and they are, that fact is accepted. If patients expect a hospital or other healthcare facility to be clean, and it is, that's accepted as standard.

It is primarily when expectations are not met—or are exceeded—that customers notice. So placing your emphasis on "value-added" service will help you achieve your internal marketing goals (or even exceed them).

EMPLOYEES ARE THE KEY

The intangible nature of services, as opposed to the tangible characteristics of products, points up that service perceptions are highly subjective. Unhappy customers cannot return services for a refund. You have one chance to meet and exceed their expectations. And because the delivery of the service requires human interaction, employees are the key to making it happen.

There is a relationship between the frequency of human interaction and the levels of satisfaction. For the most part, the more people involved in the delivery of a service, the less likely the customer will be satisfied. Therefore, the value of a well-informed, loyal and courteous staff dedicated to achieving excellence cannot be overstated.

The variability of service makes it challenging to establish and maintain performance standards and guarantee consistency in quality. For these reasons, healthcare organizations must select and train their employees carefully and exercise tight quality controls over them.

Organizational values that express commitment to customer satisfaction and employee development are the cornerstone of an internal marketing effort and can best be accomplished through value-driven performance by:

- Selecting new employees whose values parallel your organizational values;

- Orienting new employees to your mission and values;

- Educating all employees on your mission, values and goals;

- Training employees to assume their roles;

- Communicating expectations and holding employees accountable for them;

- Recognizing and rewarding employees who contribute to customer satisfaction.

SELECT QUALIFIED EMPLOYEES

Hiring the right people is the first step, but it is becoming increasingly difficult given the shortages of qualified personnel in many healthcare professions. Nonetheless, if you are to achieve a service culture that drives responsiveness to customers' needs, it is imperative that you consider whether a candidate has the necessary skills and clinical/technical and humanistic dimensions of the role.

The axiom, "the best predictor of future behavior is past behavior" holds true when it comes to the selection of employees. If you solicit behavioral examples in response to questions about how the candidate handled difficult situations in the past, you will be able to interpret how the person will handle similar situations with your customers. Interviewing that is directed to uncovering a candidate's humanism, as well as his technical aptitude and experience, will increase your chances of hiring the right person.

It is important to communicate expectations during an interview. Just as you are evaluating whether the candidate will fit into your facility, the employee should have an opportunity to assess whether this is the type of organization in which he or she would feel comfortable working. If you place importance on professional appearance and have a strict dress code (which is uniformly enforced throughout the organization), let the candidate know in advance. Express your organizational values in the interview.

ORIENT NEW EMPLOYEES

New employee orientation should be a welcoming celebration for those who have "made the cut." It should not be, as it has often become, the forum for communicating the rules and regulations. While there are plenty of safety (and other) procedures which need to be related, orientation is the time to communicate your rites and rituals, history and traditions, and what your organization dictates as it relates to employee attitudes, appearance and actions.

ALL EMPLOYEES SERVE

While you may focus your development efforts on the front-line staff, an organizational commitment to service should not exclude those who may not have direct customer contact but who serve those who do. For instance, a responsive central supply department is essential if other personnel are to be responsive to the needs of patients and physicians.

Marketing of healthcare services is a relatively new concept to employees. Employees must be knowledgeable about the goals and objectives of the marketing effort and understand the roles they play in contributing to its success. Service marketers, of course, must communicate marketing plans and programs to the employees responsible for implementing them.

TRAIN EMPLOYEES TO ASSUME THEIR ROLES

When it comes to creating a customer-responsive staff, healthcare organizations have traditionally focused attention on training programs that encourage employees to be caring and courteous. The reality is you cannot train someone to care. Caring is an inherent desire. A person either does or doesn't. What you must do is communicate expectations of performance, create management systems and practices that will reward positive contributions, develop the skills and provide the rationale for why customer service is inherent in every employee's responsibility.

Training programs that are specifically designed to develop skills and create awareness for the values and benefits of customer satisfaction can be implemented on a departmental basis, or they can be sponsored for all employees. Participation in inter-disciplinary groups will help to facilitate inter-departmental communication and cooperation.

Employees generally believe they have good customer relations skills and lecturing to them about service is a sure way to ignite their defensiveness. Therefore, it is important to encourage employees to actively participate in small and large group discussions that will encourage problem-solving. Employees are typically much better qualified than are their managers to identify obstacles that stand in the way of providing superior service and impede service performance. By involving them in the process of developing solutions and innovations, you increase their personal investment and collective commitment to achieve customer satisfaction.

ANTICIPATE RESPONSES TO PREDICTABLE INTERACTIONS

If employees are involved in repetitive, predictable interactions with customers, "scripts" can be developed to identify statements, gestures and activities that will create positive impressions. Scripting is relatively easy if you analyze the tasks and identify those key phrases and gestures that result in making the patient feel that he is a special customer. It is not enough to say to employees, "Register patients courteously." While most employees do understand the concept of courtesy, their execution of the task may not communicate the level of consideration and respect that you desire. Identify what you mean. Scripting strategic responses will help you meet and exceed customer expectations.

When developing scripts, identify the purpose of the interaction and the content of the message.
Identify:

- The interaction/service

- The purpose

- The information which should be shared with the patient

- The approaches/techniques used to meet needs

- The extra measures of service to exceed patient expectations

Anticipate:

- Questions

- Special needs

- Sources of dissatisfaction

For example, a staff member who registers a patient in an outpatient surgery center can use the following format in scripting:

1.	Acknowledge arrival	Eye contact Nod
2.	Extend greeting	"Good morning"
3.	Introduce self	"My name is_____"
4.	Establish rapport	Eye contact Smile Call patient by name
5.	Identify purpose following empathy statement	"I know that you are probably anxious to get settled but I will need to ask you a few questions. . ."
6.	Anticipate needs	"Are you comfortable?" OR "Do you have any questions?"
7.	Deliver service	Ask questions Display facial expressions Use patient's name
8.	Communicate expectations	"Thank you for your patience. Our next stop will be the lab. Dr. Smith has ordered some blood tests. I will be happy to escort you there. May I take your bags. . ." " . . . I have notified Janet that you are here. If you will have a seat in our reception area, she will be right with you."
9.	Closure	"Thank you, Mrs. Lopez. Please let any of us know if we can respond to any other questions or needs while you are here."

DEVELOP ACCOUNTABILITY

The formula for success in generating employee awareness of, participation in and commitment to customer relations is simple:

- Communicate expectations;

- Reward and recognize employees who contribute;

- Counsel and develop those who do not meet the expectations;

- Dismiss those who won't conform.

It is important to differentiate between employees who "can't" and employees who "won't" conform to meet your expectations. You have an obligation and responsibility to work with and develop an employee who demonstrates a willingness and commitment but does not have the skill or orientation to do a good job. If, however, an employee consciously sabotages your organizational effort with rude, negative, indifferent, uncooperative, defiant and contemptible behaviors, you simply cannot afford to have that person on your service delivery team. By dismissing such an employee, not only will you increase your chances of creating customer satisfaction, but you will probably enhance employee satisfaction. Employees who share your values do not appreciate the negative behavior of those who do not.

Communicate your expectations verbally and in writing by drafting standards of performance that relate to the values of customer service. Formal feedback sessions should be scheduled on a quarterly basis since annual performance evaluations are not frequent enough to provide the support and direction that encourages improvement. Informal coaching and feedback should be offered by managers and supervisors on a regular and ongoing basis.

WANDERING MANAGERS CAN PROVIDE REINFORCEMENT

Managers and administrators who wander about the facility expose themselves to many opportunities to provide informal feedback to employees. For example, if you observe an employee who is challenged by an unreasonabe, irate, agitated patient, there is an ideal opportunity to approach that staff member once he or she is alone and offer your admiration and feedback. You can say, "I saw that difficult situation a few minutes ago, and I want to let you know I thought you handled it very well." Your comment will be reinforcing and make the employee feel good.

Or you can respond by saying, "I saw you handle that patient's problem a few minutes ago. You really handled it well. You know what I particularly liked? The way you stayed calm, called the patient by name and offered some alternative solutions for her. You were really resourceful. Congratulations!" Now you have not only made the employee feel good, but you have reinforced a few of the specific techniques of complaint handling that will serve that employee well in future situations.

Of course, if you witness an employee not doing an adequate job of responding to the customer, you can approach and say, "Bob, I couldn't help but overhear you and that angry patient. That was a real challenging situation. I noticed that you tried to calm her down by staying calm yourself and using her name. Are there any other things that might have been useful in that situation?" Listen to what the employee says. Be prepared to offer some suggestions. In doing so, you are extending employee development beyond the classroom.

RECOGNIZE THOSE WHO CONTRIBUTE

As you value quality service, to customers, so you will value those employees who extend it. You should make "situational heroes" of them. Catch employees in the act of doing something nice for patients and reward them with recognition such as a coupon for a free meal or a couple of movie tickets. News of this type of spontaneous and immediate recognition will travel fast. Ask patients to identify employees who have gone out of their way to make their visit to your facility more pleasant. Seek employee nominations of colleagues who exemplify the institution's values and are cooperative, courteous and caring team members. Experiment with a little non-traditional "hoopla" to pay tribute to those contributing members of your team.

INCLUDE OTHER MEMBERS OF YOUR SERVICE TEAM

While we have concentrated on the management, motivation and development of employees, there are other members of your service delivery team who should also be included. For example, if you have volunteers on your staff, include them in your internal marketing program. Volunteers are typically highly visible within an organization. With the increasing incidence of layoffs, healthcare organizations are relying more and more on volunteers to staff front-line areas. You should have similar expectations of your voluntary employees as you do your paid staff.

Physicians and their staffs also are important members of your internal marketing team. Interestingly, research on consumer attitudes and preferences, as related in a National Research Corporation study, indicates that women have stronger preferences and opinions than men. Women consistently rate such characteristics as physician concern, telephone access, reasonable fees, appointment convenience, flexible payment and hours, personal concern and friendliness as being more important than do men.[1]

Consumers have rated physicians' interest in them as the most important factor in selecting and continuing to use a physician. On a scale of one to ten, in a research study conducted by the previously cited National Research Corporation and reported in *Modern Healthcare* magazine (January 17, 1986), consumers rated "physician concern for patients" an average mean score of 9.61.[2]

The staffs of physicians are important too. In a public opinion poll sponsored by the American Medical Association, 75 percent of the respondents said that "the way I am treated by the doctor's staff" is very important as a reason to keep a personal physician. When physicians are aware of your internal marketing program, it is likely they will want to also involve their own employees. You can encourage physician awareness of and participation in your internal marketing program by involving their employees in your indoctrinations.[3]

WORD OF MOUTH ADVERTISING INFLUENCES IMAGE

Research indicates that when a customer is satisfied with a service, she will tell four to five other people. If the customer is dissatisfied, she will tell approximately ten other people! Of those dissatisfied customers, 13 percent will tell 20 other people.[4]

You can invest a lot of money in advertising, but the testimonials shared in informal conversations will carry more weight with your customers. Women ask other women for advice about their own medical problems and those of their family. And the answers they receive influence the decisions they make.

MONITOR SATISFACTION

One of the most important aspects of an internal marketing program is the way you monitor satisfaction. Certainly, instruments that tell you the extent to which you are meeting customer's expectations will enable you to better manage the delivery of your service. One such tool is a questionnaire designed to measure key elements of satisfaction. Were procedures explained adequately? Was the staff responsive to their needs? Were they friendly and considerate? Questionnaires should be designed to monitor satisfaction and diagnose problems.

While questionnaires are relatively inexpensive and easy to develop and administer, consider some other ways to solicit feedback from your customers. For instance, just as focus groups can be used to uncover customer preferences and needs during market research, similar groups can be assembled to uncover information relating to how well you satisfy the needs and expectations of the users of your services.

Telephone and personal interviews are also useful, especially while the customer is in your facility. Yet, healthcare consumers may be reluctant to report dissatisfactions while they are hospitalized for fear of retaliation. Take this into consideration if you are soliciting informal feedback from in-patients. Customers who are utilizing services on an out-patient basis may reveal more information. Encourage managers to talk with patients about levels of satisfaction and dissatisfaction.

WELCOME COMPLAINTS

If your organization is truly customer-responsive, expect an increase in the number of complaints you receive.

Many people equate the absence of complaints with an absence of dissatisfaction. The absence of complaints, however, is a sign that your customers may be so intimidated by the system they avoid telling you about their problems! But if they're not talking to *you*, they will surely be telling *others*.

Once a patient leaves your facility, your ability to correct the problem and restore confidence and loyalty will be dramatically decreased. This has a significant effect on what the customer will tell others and also determines if she will return to your institution. During the Carter Administration, the White House Office of Consumer Affairs retained a company named Technical Assistance Research Programs, Inc., to study consumer behavior. Among TARP's findings were the following[5]:

- The average business never hears from 96 percent of its unhappy customers. For every complaint received, the average company has 26 customers with problems.

- Complainers are more likely than noncomplainers to do

business again with the company that upset them, even if the problem isn't satisfactorily resolved.

- Of the customers who register a complaint, between 54 and 70 percent will do business again with the organization if their complaint is resolved. That figure goes up to 95 percent if the customer feels that the complaint was resolved quickly.

- Customers who have complained to an organization and have had their complaints satisfactorily resolved tell an average of five people about the treatment they received.

No one likes to be at the receiving end of a complaint. Soliciting complaints is threatening to most employees unless they're educated properly in how to respond to them. Actually, complaints can be one of your most important and meaningful internal marketing resource tools.

When you receive information about dissatisfaction, it is important to qualify and quantify it. For example, are some complaints repetitive? If so, analyze why.

A complaint is simply an *an expression of dissatisfaction.* In cases of repetitive complaints, you should analyze whether the expectations of the complainer are realistic or unrealistic. If the latter, explain to the patient what can rightfully be done about her problem.

If an unmet expectation is realistic, however, direct your efforts toward preventing future complaints.

For example, repetitive complaints about delays require closer examination: is the problem caused by poor communication between departments? Is the amount of time allowed for each examination or consultation sufficient? Can you revise the procedures?

Often, some situations that give rise to many complaints simply cannot be resolved or prevented. When confronted with such dilemmas, your best course of action is to inform the customer about the reasons for the delay. People are more patient about waiting when they know the reasons for it—and are kept informed. Failure to respond quickly to a complaint may again fuel the frustration and anger of the patient, often out of proportion to the original situation that precipitated it.

Acknowledge written complaints immediately. A telephone call, preferably from the person to whom the complaint was addressed (or someone of similar authority), should be made within three days. You may need to investigate further. Simply let the customer know that you are aware of the problem, you are investigating it, and, if it is appropriate, that you will be contacting her later. It helps if you can offer a specific time when you'll call again. Finally, thank the customer for letting you know of her dissatisfaction.

EVALUATE YOUR SYSTEMS

Policies and procedures define the protocols and rules of your healthcare service delivery system. Customer-oriented organizations want to reduce the regulations that are barriers to effective customer service. In highly regulated and critical industries such as healthcare, rules are often, by necessity, frustrating to the customer—and many times to those who must enforce them.

In such situations, every attempt should be made to explain the reasons for the rules so customers understand the rationale behind them.

Analyze your policies and procedures to ensure that such rules are not made solely for the convenience of the staff. A customer-oriented facility is truly one which considers the customer's comfort, convenience and care *first*.

The service orientation of the healthcare facility also means that you must empower your employees to make decisions in the best interest of the customer. All too often, organizations tie the hands of employees by making them accountable for enforcing rules, rather than making it possible for them to judiciously circumvent rules on occasion to benefit the customer.

CONCLUSION

We all know the cliché—"You can bring a horse to water, but you can't make him drink." And, as with all clichés, it's true, especially so in healthcare. No amount of well-conceived, beautifully executed, skillfully implemented external marketing efforts can sustain goodwill and encourage consumer satisfaction if, once through your doors, the patient's expectations are unfulfilled. Advertising may be the sizzle, but the real marketing, one-on-one inside your organization, is the steak.

In order for a patient to be satisfied, you need to have both—the sizzle to attract her to your healthcare facility and the steak to please her with quality Tender Loving Care once she's inside.

NOTES

1. Jensen, Joyce and Ned Miklovic, "Consumers Cite Physicians' Interest As Most Important Factor in Selection," *Modern Healthcare,* January 17, 1986, pp. 48-50.

2. Ibid, pp. 48-50.

3. "Attitudes on Healthcare Issues," American Medical Association, 1984.

4. Tarp, Inc., "Measuring the Grapevine: Consumer Response and Word-of-Mouth," The Coca-Cola Company, Atlanta, GA., 1981.

5. Ibid.

APPENDIX: FOCUS GROUP
STUDY REPORT

I n the field of healthcare, women have been short-changed. With specialized needs and as the primary decision makers for their own and their families' healthcare, women are a virtually untapped market. Women's Health Centers of America have taken the first steps to address this market through the development of healthcare centers aimed at meeting the unique health needs of women.

In July of 1985, primary and secondary market research was conducted to determine the optimum position for entry into the San Diego market by

Women's Health Centers of America. Primary research consisted of focus groups held in San Diego on the nights of July 17 and 18. Secondary research consisted of an on-line database search of existing competition, a periodical review and logo/symbol search. The research was carried out by York/Alpern, Inc., for Women's Health Centers.

GOALS

The primary goal of this study was to define the appropriate market position for Women's Health Centers. This included a definition of the target market, of the product and of a brand name/identity for the centers.

The results have been compiled into this report and an accompanying videotape.

POSITIONING STATEMENT

Women's Health Centers provide sensitive and comprehensive medical care designed for and by women.

Women are angry and tired of uncaring doctors and insensitive staff who they feel spend too little time with them for too much money. Time and time again, our focus group participants expressed the desire to be treated as individuals, to have their problems listened to in an unhurried atmosphere by warm and caring medical professionals. As one participant said:

I know the reason I put off seeing the gynecologist for a year or two at a time is because when I get in there it's just terrible. You're just made to feel like you're not exactly there for a nice chat. You go in and you disrobe and you get a little paper blanket to put over you and that's it. The air conditioner's on, you're freezing to death, the doctor takes his time, and I don't like it. I'm very uncomfortable anyway. I don't particularly enjoy that type of thing, and they don't make it any nicer. They really don't.

These women perceive their needs as special and as different from both men's and children's health needs. Women are interested in comprehensive care, not just gynecological services, administered by women physicians and staff.

Primary Market

Women between the ages of 30 and 50, with teenage daughters, using third-party payers, and who work outside the home.

An overwhelming majority of the focus group participants said that they wanted a woman gynecologist and more sensitive healthcare for their daughters than they (the participant) got or were getting. A center with a warm environment, sensitive to the fears and needs of young girls dealing with menstruation and puberty, coupled with the mother's desire to "do better for my daughter," would provide a relatively easy entry point into this market. The following quotations from our participants illustrate this point:

> . . . I've sworn up and down if I have girls, which I do—I have two now—that when they first experience any kind of problems or start their periods and have problems, I would take them to a woman and/or some kind of clinic. I would like to see some kind of doctors that are geared to younger girls that are scared.

> I pray and hope that by the time my daughter experiences these problems, that maybe there's someone out there that is more inclined to help young girl's through this problem . . .

Once captured, women demonstrate extreme loyalty to their physician. When the teenage girl is happy with her healthcare, Women's Health Centers is in a position to keep her as a "Customer-for-Life."

The likelihood of the mother switching to the Center for her own care would be influenced directly by the level of dissatisfaction with her current healthcare and by the positive experience of her daughter(s).

Women older and younger than this group were excluded from the primary market for several reasons. Older women are more set in their ways and are most likely to be satisfied and comfortable with their medical care. They are not looking for an alternative and are not likely to be influenced by their grown daughters' choice of treatment center or physician.

Younger women are often influenced by their mothers' choices and are not heavy users of medical care. Without long-term experience in the marketplace, the under 30 group is not aware of the need or desirability of an alternative. Members of this group who have a high degree of contact with the medical system are most likely to use obstetric and pediatric physicians, two specialties which will not be represented at Women's Health Center.

THE PRODUCT

Staffing

> Women's Health Centers will be staffed solely by women. Nurse practitioners may be used, as long as they are women.

The attitude of the staff is the single most important factor for women when choosing healthcare. A sensitive and caring attitude and a willingness to spend time and communicate with the patient were cited as what women want most from their healthcare. Women clinicians, whether physician, nurse practitioner or nursing staff, are perceived as being most likely to embody this attitude. As one woman explained it:

> I feel like at my doctor, I wasn't thrilled with things with

him, but all the people at his office and his particular nurse—she was so helpful. I called her and she talked to me on the phone a long time after I had my baby and I was having problems, and she called me back to see how I was doing, and when I go in, she would answer questions for me, she'd talk to me, and she's the one who would do my blood pressure and the weight and all that, and because of her I felt more comfortable. There was somebody I could talk to, and she had children and could relate to it. I think she'd have been better off being my doctor, from what she did compared to what he did. It made a big difference.

Most of the participants had only positive experiences with nurse practitioners and expressed at least a willingness, if not a preference, to use them again. Again, it was more a function of attitude rather than credentials that was important to them, as illustrated in the following quotation:

From being in the hospital, I think that the nurses are doing much more than the doctor is doing. You see them more, you rely on them more, they answer your questions, and I think—my doctor has got so many patients he doesn't even take new ones and he doesn't have time for the ones that he has. I'd rather go to somebody that maybe tries harder, that cares a little more. If that's a nurse practitioner, that's fine with me.

DESCRIPTION

For these women comprehensive medical care means more than offering a range of medical specialties. Diagnostics, informational services, special programs, as well as several medical specialties were mentioned as essential components of a "comprehensive" care center. In the words of one participant:

... what I want is to have the labs, different physicians for different things, all in one building, have a lot of litera-

ture, have classes offered that you can sign up for at different times, whether it's nutrition or gynecological
things . . . If everything could be in one spot and they get
to know you, your records are there, and they've got different people to take care of different things, I think I'd
probably go more often, and I'd feel better taking my
daughter there too.

Obstetrics, while important, is not an essential service.
Many women discussed the inconvenience of having to wait for
a physician to deliver a baby, and expressed an interest in a center that would offer gynecological and ancillary services only.

Specialties that were mentioned and for which a high level
of use was indicated were: dermatology, allergy, and counseling. All three of these are perceived as services seldom offered
to women yet needed the most by them.

A center would not be perceived as comprehensive without diagnostic services. Those specific services mentioned as
essential are: laboratory services, radiology and ultrasound.
Most participants did not think that it was really important to
have the "most" modern equipment or state-of-the-art technology. However, it is also clear that the participants do not
understand the value of having or the implications of *not* having
that type of equipment/service available.

Informational services are an essential ingredient to the
success of a comprehensive health center for women. Women
continually expressed both frustration and displeasure at the
unavailability and lack of good, reliable medical information.
Informational brochures, videotapes, seminars (for a nominal
fee), a library and a physical referral service were all mentioned
as appealing components of an information service. As our participants stated:

Everybody wants a choice, and I think everybody just
wants to be more educated, either to have somebody sit
down or to be able to send you to a class or something to
explain what your options are and what is available . . .

Her (female doctor)office had lots of brochures, informative information. He (male doctor) had nothing like that. If I was going to a woman's center I would hope they would have a lot of things to keep me informed on the newer things that are happening, keep me up to date.

In particular, seminars were mentioned as a good vehicle to attract mother/daughter visits and to introduce them to the center.

Our focus group participants also expressed an interest in a variety of special programs about health issues of particular concern to women. These programs would serve the dual purpose of being both educational and profitable. Specifically mentioned were programs on: PMS, osteoporosis, stress reduction, nutritional counseling, weight control, sports medicine and baseline mammography.

PHYSICAL OPERATION

Women's Health Centers will offer: extended hours, convenient location, ample parking and a soft, comfortable and clean environment. Waiting time will be kept to a minimum and current information on healthcare will be available for the clients' use. It will be a policy to notify clients of any change or delay in their scheduled appointment time.

For working women, extended hours are essential. Many cannot or will not take the time away from work for healthcare, either their own or their daughters'. Many women also indicated that they may use health services more often were they available at more convenient times. As one woman so aptly put it:

For myself, I would make an appointment more readily. Lots of times I just put it off and put it off and put it off because it takes all day.

Women do not expect or desire a costly or fancy environment for their health services. What they do expect is a comfortable, clean, home-like environment, with soft lighting and access to current information. One woman described it as:

Something soft, comfortable. I think that when people say that decor doesn't make any difference, I don't think they realize what different kind of testing you've been through or anything like that. People have immediate reactions to it, especially when they're under stress or come into a room. I think the lighting has a tremendous amount to do with it. It doesn't have to be ultra-fancy, just comfortable.

Participants expressed a desire for access to informational material (library and videotapes) to use during the waiting time.

A convenient location with ample parking was mentioned often as part of an ideal health center.

ADVERTISING

Specific Objectives

- To introduce the concept of comprehensive, one-stop medical care exclusively for women

- To encourage awareness among the primary market of the existence of an alternative preferable to their traditionally male-oriented, male-delivered healthcare

- To build brand awareness with Women's Health Centers of America as distinct from other women's health centers

Attributes to be Communicated

- A sensitive staff attitude

- Comprehensive care, i.e. a complete diagnostic information and treatment center

- Administered by women, for women

- A better way to introduce adolescent girls to feminine healthcare in a low-threat, sensitive environment

- A competent staff, i.e. credentials

- Convenience: extended hours, convenient location, ample parking, short waiting time, notification of cancellation or time change of appointment

- Comfort: comfortable, home-like decor, clean, friendly atmosphere

Media

Local radio spots, the yellow pages, direct mail and presentations will be used to promote Women's Health Centers.

By far the most effective method of advertising women's healthcare is word-of-mouth. Almost without exception, the participants said that the recommendation of a friend is the most important referral source they used and the most important factor in deciding whether to try a particular doctor. Every contact between patient and staff is not only a point of delivery of quality medical care, but a marketing contact as well. The patient that is treated well today will return tomorrow and most likely recommend the center to a friend. As one woman put it:

I would talk around with different friends to see if they had gone to that particular doctor, and if I knew of somebody with a particular disorder, I would see who my friends went to that had this particular problem.

Advertising can serve to enhance the effectiveness of word-of-mouth as well as to penetrate those areas where word-of-mouth has not yet reached.

Direct mail is an excellent vehicle for advertising Women's Health Centers. Heavy mailings of brochures and invitations for special tours and seminars are an effective way to bring potential clients into the Center.

Our focus group participants expressed a distaste for healthcare advertisements on television. Many women look to the Yellow Pages for a source of healthcare services and none expressed a negative feeling about that vehicle for advertising.

Several women mentioned that a presentation through their insurance carrier at work would be a valuable and informative way of introducing the Women's Center. Radio stations, with the appropriate demographics, would be an effective way to reach potential clients. Print would also be an effective media, but the perceived intent must be informational rather than a "hard sell" approach.

THINGS TO AVOID

Use of the words, or allusions to:

- Feminist

- Lesbian

- Clinic

- Alternative

- Price

- Scolding or judgmental approach

Clinic connotes for most women a broader range of services than what Women's Health Centers are interested in providing. As one woman described it:

> I would think a clinic would mean that they would have to have all of the services available, other than surgery. To locate a particular problem, they'd have to have x-ray, a laboratory, pharmacy, physicians on duty that would be trained to aid any form of illness if it's a women's clinic; if it's a clinic as such, I would think that's what "clinic" would be, involving all of it, so that you wouldn't have to go anywhere else.

Use of the word alternative still holds a 60s meaning for many participants and implies a service that is on the fringe, or not in the mainstream. One of our participants said:

> "It's alternative. I mean, I'm really for alternative things, but there's just something about something—alternative medicine, that I still haven't accepted, I guess."

Price is *not* an issue for women in their choice of healthcare services. Any mention of price is perceived as "sleazy" or suspect, as most women feel that one way or another, a service will charge what it needs to make money.

As a group, women are tired of the male-oriented, paternal approach to healthcare. They do not want to be patronized, judged or scolded for their behavior or health practices. Any paternalistic attitudes in staff or advertising will be sure to alienate women clients.

GRAPHIC DESIGN

Those symbols which elicited a favorable response were those which were characterized by a circle or circular design incorporating a symbol of caring or nurturing, such as hands, a heart, or touching. Any symbol showing softness or traditional femininity, such as a flower, was also well-received.

The symbols which were disliked by a majority of the participants were those which were angular, simple graphic designs connotating femininity, such as the biological symbol for female, which is currently being used by Women's Health Centers of America.

SUGGESTED NAMES

The following is a list of suggested names for the new Women's Health Centers:

- Women's Medical Group of San Diego
- San Diego Medical Center for Women
- Women's Health and Medical Resource Center
- For Women, By Women
- National Women's Centers
- Women's Centers of America
- Women's Comprehensive Care Centers

CONCLUSION

From this study on women's healthcare, we can define a clear market position and entry point to introduce Women's Health Centers to the San Diego area. A description of the product to be offered, guidelines for an effective advertising campaign, as well as suggestions for a logo and name, are included. The highlights of this report are outlined below.

- Women's Health Centers provide sensitive and comprehensive medical care designed for and by women.
- The primary target will be women between the ages of 30 and 50, with teenage daughters, who use third-party payers and who work outside of the home.
- Women's Health Centers will be staffed solely by

women. Nurse practitioners (women also) may be included.

- The range of services will include Diagnostics, Informational Services, Special Programs, and several Medical specialties.

- Obstetrics will not be included.

- Women's Health Centers will offer:
    extended hours
    ample parking
    convenient location
    clean and comfortable environment
    short waiting time

- Women's Health Centers will be promoted through local radio spots, the yellow pages, direct mail and presentations.

Answers to
Who Created What?
A Challenge for Sexist Thinkers:

What you don't know can hurt you
was written by a woman.

Don't believe everything you fear
was created by a man.

INDEX

www.ingramcontent.com/pod-product-compliance
Lightning Source LLC
Chambersburg PA
CBHW031055180526
45163CB00002BA/850